The **Teach** ▮▮▮▮▮▮▮▮▮

MW01058175

Jim Burke

Content Area Reading

How to:

- Boost Student Comprehension of All Texts
- Engage Students as Strategic Readers
- Improve Memory of Key Information

◢ SCHOLASTIC

Dedication:

To America's newest teachers

(page 27) Excerpt from page 913 of *World History: Patterns of Interaction*. Copyright © 1999. Used by permission of Holt McDougal, a division of Houghton Mifflin Harcourt.

Series Editor: Lois Bridges

Designer: Maria Lilja

Production Editor: Gloria Pipkin

Proofreader: Eileen Judge

Cover Photo: Bruce Forrester

Interior Photos: Jim Burke

ISBN 13: 978-0-439-93449-7

ISBN 10: 0-439-93449-4

Scholastic Inc. grants teachers permission to photocopy the activity and stationery pages from this book for classroom use only. No other part of this publication may be reproduced in whole or in part, or stored in a retrieval system, or transmitted in any form or by any means, electronic, mechanical, photocopying, recording, or otherwise, without written permission of the publisher. For information regarding permission, write to Scholastic Inc., 557 Broadway, New York, NY 10012.

Copyright © 2009 by Jim Burke

All rights reserved. Published by Scholastic Inc.

Printed in the U.S.A.

1 2 3 4 5 6 7 8 9 10   23   14 13 12 11 10 09

Contents

Introduction

"Literacy involves the ability to encode or decode meaning in any of the symbolic forms used in the culture."
—Eliot Eisner, "Preparing for Today and Tomorrow," *Educational Leadership*

I teach students in developmental reading classes, college prep, and Advanced Placement English classes. In these classes, all students struggle at one time or another with various types of text—or at least they should. If we assign texts that offer no challenge, it's not likely our students will develop the skills, strength, or fluency they need for powerful reading across content areas. While the students in my college prep freshmen English class seem, in so many obvious ways, different from the students in my senior AP Literature class, they face a common challenge: both groups routinely encounter texts that resist easy understanding. Their history and science classes, for example, require them to read an array of texts: Web sites, maps, primary source documents, infotexts such as charts and graphs, photographs, and, of course, more traditional texts such as speeches, textbooks, and articles on issues related to health, science, or history.

In other words, reading is a daily demand, one that is fundamental to students' success in school (and, of course, beyond). Such literacy demands only get more complex as students get older. A report published by the Alliance for Excellent Education sums up the challenge best:

> After the elementary years, not only do reading assignments become longer and more full of content, they also become increasingly *varied* in their style, vocabulary, text structure, purpose, and intended audience.... Middle and high school students must learn that in some classes they are expected to follow written instructions to the letter, while in others they are expected to read skeptically, or to question the author's assumptions, or to analyze the writer's style. Moving from one subject area to the next, they must tap into entirely different sets of vocabulary and background knowledge.... To enter into any academic discipline is to become comfortable with its ways of looking at and communicating about the world (Heller and Greenleaf 2007, p.7).

When it comes to reading, we know so much more today about what kids need and how to teach it; what's more, as the result of various reforms, schools and teachers are now held accountable for the success of all students. What does this mean for those of us who walk into the class every day to teach our subject—English, math, history, science, health—to thirty or more students, many of whom are English learners, students with special needs, struggling or disengaged readers? We must be more strategic and effective in teaching students how to read those texts they will face in class and on state exams. This addition to the *Teacher's Essential Guide* series offers you core strategies, each based on reliable research, which you can use efficiently in your class to help all students read your content with greater skill and confidence and, in this way, develop the skills they need to succeed as students, citizens, and future employees.

Content Area Reading Self-Assessment

For each of the items below, record an answer between 1 and 5.

1 Never   **2** Rarely   **3** Sometimes   **4** Usually   **5** Always

After completing this self-assessment, identify those areas with most urgent need of attention and improvement. For each statement to which your response was "never," "rarely," or "sometimes," go to the corresponding chapter and learn what you can do to improve in that area.

Understand the Reading Process

☐ I prepare students to read by using a variety of strategies before they read.

☐ I ensure that students are active readers by having them apply a range of techniques during the reading process.

☐ I teach students how to evaluate, reflect on, and refine their performance after they read.

Teach Students to Be Strategic Readers

☐ My students know how to identify the main idea and supporting details in whatever type of text they read.

☐ My students and I use a variety of strategies to develop and access their background knowledge as it relates to the texts they read.

☐ My students learn to ask a variety of questions throughout the reading process about the different types of text they read.

☐ My students employ a range of strategies to help them visualize what they read.

continued on next page

Use a Range of Instructional Strategies to Enhance and Extend Comprehension

☐ My students use writing before, during, and after they read to improve their comprehension and retention of what they read.

☐ We use discussion throughout the reading process to increase engagement, improve comprehension, and aid memory.

☐ We read aloud texts during the reading process.

☐ I use think-alouds to improve reading comprehension and use of strategies.

☐ I use graphic organizers to help students understand and analyze what they read.

☐ I use a variety of techniques to help students visually represent their thinking about the content of the texts they read.

☐ I create and ask my students to use different anticipation guides throughout the reading process.

☐ I model for students what they should do as effective readers throughout the reading process.

☐ I incorporate a variety of performances to help students engage with, understand, and remember what they read.

1. Understand the Reading Process

Watching artists begin a drawing is intriguing. Some start with what you eventually realize is the nose, others with some slant of what becomes the jaw, others with what we soon recognize as an eye. The point is that all artists have their own way of approaching the task, one that works for them and helps them bring to life the subject they are trying to understand for themselves and convey it to others accurately and clearly. As readers, we are not much different when it comes to our own idiosyncratic processes. Some of us ask certain types of questions before we begin, others make connections, still others find ways to "see" what they are reading, using a variety of techniques to help them visualize. Of course, there are those readers who have not developed a useful process for themselves; for these readers, their process is something like hitting the play button on a movie they don't know the title of, which they then watch with their back to the screen and with the sound turned off. In other words, they have a process, but it's flawed or even counterproductive, and results in little pleasure and less understanding.

Guiding Principles

- **Prepare to read by setting a purpose and choosing a strategy before reading.**
- **Keep the purpose and plan in mind while reading.**
- **Reflect on the results and reread as necessary to improve comprehension and memory after reading.**

No one these days questions the validity or the value of thinking of writing as a process. *Writing as process* makes sense and is consistent with our own experience. Writing, however, is observable, public—we can see what we are doing on the page. Reading, on the other hand, is a private process, one taking place in the workshop of our mind, only yielding evidence of success or trouble when we finally take a test or write about or discuss the text in class. When a student in my AP English class offers a hilarious but totally invalid misreading of a poem about whippoorwills, assuming (as he later explained) that a whippoorwill is an electronic bug zapper on the back porch, something terribly wrong has happened during his process, something he was unable to recognize and remedy. In that case, then, we discuss his reading process and the steps he followed to arrive at that amusing interpretation. If we consider his first reading as the writer's equivalent of a *draft* of his final interpretation, one that is subject to revision, it opens up the process. It renders more public the process we use to make sense of what we read and disabuses students of the notion of a "reading gene" or any other such belief that reading is something you either get or don't, can do—or can't.

The following model of a reading process offers just one way of looking at this idea of reading. It is not meant to be a lock-step process; rather, it is flexible, offering teachers and students a way to approach reading while they identify and refine those steps in their own processes. Because we read a range of text types—literary and informational, visual and symbolic, media and print—we need a process that we can adapt to any of these different texts, refining and changing it in whatever ways are necessary to make sense of a particular text in the context of a specific task.

Prepare to read by setting a purpose and choosing a strategy before reading.

These stages in the reading process are not for students alone: each one applies to teachers as well. Just as students must establish a purpose for reading a given text, so, too, must teachers consider their own purpose in choosing and assigning each text. Why this text—and for this class? Or why have them read this text one way (e.g., to identify the author's main ideas about global warming) as opposed to reading it with another, more advanced purpose in mind (e.g., to identify how the author uses evidence and rhetoric to persuade the reader). In this chapter, however, we will focus on what teachers can do to develop students' reading process since our goal here is to teach students to be independent, effective readers of both informational and literary texts. In this chapter, I mention certain ideas in the context of the reading process, which I discuss in much greater detail in subsequent chapters in the context of reading strategies. For now, let us look at a variety of ways teachers can prepare students prior to turning them loose to read the assigned text:

Teach students to develop a purpose question (PQ) appropriate to the subject, text, and unit of study. Such questions transform a passive, linear approach to reading into an interactive, recursive process in which students evaluate information in light of their purpose. In my freshman class, I organize the units of study around larger guiding questions such as "What is success, and how can we achieve it?" Thus when we read individual texts, whether they are short stories, essays, poems, or Web sites, we formulate a PQ specific to the text at hand. If it is an introductory article about the Trojan War in a textbook, we take the title and turn it into a PQ such as "What was the Trojan War?" Since we are reading it as background knowledge prior to reading *The Odyssey*, this is an appropriate, useful question; were I a social studies teacher, however, teaching kids about ancient Greece, I might ask a different question more suitable to my subject, such as, "What led to the Trojan War, and how is it similar to or different from the wars we have fought in modern times?" Crafting a good PQ takes some practice. To this end, when I first introduce the PQ, we generate questions together; later, after some initial success, students develop their own, which we then put on the board and, through collaborative discussion, refine into a good PQ we all agree is useful. Finally, the students make their own PQs once they show they know how.

> (PQ = PURPOSE QUESTION)
>
> PQ: 1. What kind of a person is Kevin Smith?
> 2. How do you know he is that kind of a person? (Underline details that support your claim)
> 3. What did Kevin Smith love to do?
> 4. What do you love to do?

Preview the text to get some sense of its difficulty and demands. If you're reading an informational text, have students scan the pages to see what features (e.g., color, captions, figures, layout) are used to organize and convey the meaning. A quick glance at the pages will also give students a sense of how long it might take them to read this text. Ask them to take, let's say, two minutes to skim the text and jot down three things they noticed or learned about the subject and what the author is saying about it. An easy variation is to have students follow these same steps and then call out their gleanings, which I list on the board, asking them, finally, to make predictions about the text based on what they know so far.

Choose a strategy or note-taking technique that reflects students' reading purpose and instructional needs. Because of the nature of the text and reading task, I may decide that the students need to learn how to take notes in a more traditional way and so will assign (and teach them to use) something like Cornell notes. Another text may serve as a preparation for a subsequent writing assignment in which I am teaching them to compare and contrast ideas, in which case I will use a more structured note-taking tool like a Venn diagram or another tool designed to help them organize details into two columns. A more difficult text might merit a more collaborative strategy that requires students to read a bit, then pause and identify the main idea and supporting details of each paragraph, annotating the text as they move through it.

Generate questions and connections related to the subject and purpose question. When you take the time to activate background knowledge or otherwise prepare the brain to learn or remember material, you increase the likelihood of comprehension and retention. Think of the mind as similar to the soil you need to prepare if you hope a plant will take root and thrive.

- How does the weather in the story reflect the tune that the author is trying to set?
- What is the purpose of having a story within a story?
- How does point of view strengthen the author's point?
- What is the significance of the story starting & ending w/ the maid & gardener?
- How does tone & structure contribute to the author's meaning?
- What makes a "classic story" aim. Fairytale
- How does the remote location contribute the themes of the story.
- How is the objective POV similar to reality?
- How does the objective pt. of view force the reader to interpret the words?
- What does the language barrier (letting in the reader but not Jig) show about their relationship?

Some questions at this stage play a crucial role in determining importance when reading. These and other more global questions about the subject can be put onto poster paper or the board and kept up for a few days; you can also keep it up longer, adding new information or questions to the poster as the unit progresses or the novel unfolds.

Determine not just the PQ but the purpose of the text in general. Every writer comes to the task with some objective in mind. If he doesn't want to entertain, he hopes to persuade; if not to persuade, then to describe or explain a process or product. Whatever the author's purpose, readers should learn to determine what it is and how the author chooses and organizes information to achieve it.

Keep the purpose and plan in mind while reading.

While they read, students need to learn to monitor their comprehension and identify those key details that will help them answer their PQ. If they find themselves confused or otherwise struggling, they need to learn how to evaluate those troubles and resolve them by refining or changing their strategies, a phase of the process that requires constant vigilance. Throughout the process of reading, students must not only apply the strategies or note-taking techniques but also evaluate how effective they are and adjust them accordingly. In addition, effective readers are also making connections—to themselves, the world, and other texts or subjects they've studied—using and adding to their background knowledge to help them understand

Zack not only reads a book he chose—Kobe Bryant's biography— but generates his own PQs so he reads to answer his questions.

and remember what they read. So much of this work goes on in the black box of the reader's brain, but during this part of the reading process, students can do many things that improve comprehension and contribute to subsequent retention:

Apply and evaluate the effectiveness of a technique as students read. To do this, periodically interrupt students' reading process to ask them to write about, discuss, or otherwise reflect on what they are doing and how it is or is not helping them. Model how to use the note-taking technique or reading strategy. This might mean projecting a sample of the handout on an overhead or

SMART Board and filling it in as students read along with you, annotating your own actions with comments to clarify what you are doing and why. In the event that you find the technique is not helping, evaluate whether it is, in fact, the right choice. If it is, you may need to adjust how you are using it; if it is not the right approach, replace it with a new, more suitable technique.

Gather information relevant to the PQ. This means taking notes in some form—on sticky notes, in the margins, or in a notebook—while reading to answer your PQ by the time you finish. In my freshman English class, for example, students read portions of *The Odyssey* guided by the PQ, "What obstacles did Odysseus encounter, and how did he overcome them?" I give them a structured note-taking sheet I created that asks them to identify the problem, its effects, and Odysseus's response and solution to the problem. In my AP English class, students reading *Hamlet* do so through one of several critical theories (e.g., Marxist, gender studies, New Criticism) and thus take notes appropriate to a PQ such as, "In what ways does gender contribute to or reveal insights about *Hamlet*?" During the reading of the play, I check students' notes and talk with them to be sure they understand what to look for when "reading for gender" and to assess the quality of their notes as they relate to answering the PQ when they finish.

Make connections as they read to increase engagement, aid comprehension, and improve retention of the details in the text. You can facilitate these connections by posing questions or asking students to use graphic organizers or visual representations of the material. In my AP English class, while students read *Oedipus Rex*, in which the state faces a crisis and the citizens appeal to Oedipus to save them, I have students read an article from the newspaper about this country's financial crisis and make connections between Oedipus and the Secretary of the Treasury. This allows students to draw on their knowledge of economics and government, both of which they are studying in other classes and which, for some, are clearly more interesting than literature. In a Contemporary World History class at my school, students read Greg Mortenson's book *Three Cups of Tea: One Man's Mission to Promote Peace . . . One School at a Time* to study Afghanistan, making connections between the author's experience there and accounts students read in their textbook and in newspapers. These connections between the real and the academic help make the lessons more concrete, more personal, since students can compare their own experiences as students with those of students in Afghanistan. In general, connections come in three flavors: text-to-self, text-to-world, and text-to-text. In the latter, students might make connections between the text they are reading and those they have already studied in your class or in another class.

Use and supplement background knowledge throughout the reading process. As students read, they inevitably encounter words, subjects, and scenarios they don't understand due to a lack of background knowledge. During the reading process, students need to learn how to assess their own understanding and identify the source of their confusion. In one class, for example, students thought they could skip past the word *midwife*, but it kept appearing; finally, they realized it was central to the meaning of the text and someone called out, "What the heck is a *midwife* anyway?!" Other situations are more demanding, such as when students reading a novel like *The Grapes of Wrath* by Steinbeck find themselves struggling with certain aspects of the story because they don't know about the Depression or the Dust Bowl, which forced many people off their farms and out west where they (along with my own relatives) hoped they could rebuild their lives in a more hospitable environment. To provide background on this era and these events, teachers bring in material from a range of sources, including photographs by Dorothea Lange, articles, and letters from individuals who survived those years.

Monitor comprehension and repair as needed. As mentioned above, students need to pay attention to their comprehension, evaluating how well they understand what they are reading in general and how the text addresses their PQ in particular. Asking students to take notes, fill out graphic organizers, or answer study questions as they read helps them monitor their comprehension and identify what they do not understand so they can get help. In my class, I often ask students to generate questions about the ideas they do not understand, asking them to identify the specific spots in the text where they get lost. Some teachers have students keep sticky notes in hand as they read so they can post questions and identify confusion right at the point where their comprehension breaks down. On these sticky notes, students write questions they have or identify what they think is the cause of their confusion at that point, and then bring these to class to get help during discussions or conferences with the teacher. During these whole-class or private discussions, the teacher asks questions such as, "What did you write on the sticky notes?" Such discussions, as well as the sticky notes themselves, become a useful, informal means of assessment teachers can use to gauge understanding and make decisions about how to adjust instruction if needed.

Reflect on the results and reread as necessary to improve comprehension and memory after reading.

After students finish reading, the process continues, much like it does after a big competition when coaches and players get together to evaluate their performance in light of their objectives. They look at the game tapes, check out the times, and study the statistics, measuring them against what they expected and asking which of the strategies were most effective, in which ways, and why. They don't want success to be an accident—it should be something they can repeat next time through intelligent application of the right techniques. If they lost, the same process of reflection will, they hope, yield insights into how they can avoid a loss next time and thereby improve both their game and their standing. Reading is very much a performance, one that merits no less reflection than an athlete's performance at a swim meet, baseball game, or tennis match. After students finish the assigned reading, they know where they are and what they did (or didn't do) to get there. Now is the time to ask the difficult questions—and to study performance in light of the results. Such reflection, however, is not built into students' process, so it requires us to make time for them to consider it. After students finish reading, teachers should make time to have students do the following:

Answer their original purpose question to evaluate their success. Whether it's a quick reading in class or a more extended reading experience such as a novel, now is the time to have students evaluate how well they understood the text. Can they answer the PQ? How fully? How accurately? After having students write down or discuss their initial understanding, I need to determine the degree of their success. Some students clearly read and understand the text well, as is reflected by their precise, detailed answers; others, however, have some gaps in their understanding and may even offer interpretations that suggest some misreadings (e.g., "You thought a whippoorwill was a *what?!*"). During this phase, I am often asking questions to assess both their understanding and their needs so I can decide what they need next. They may, at this point, take a quiz, or write a structured response (e.g., "What were Odysseus's problems and how did he solve them in this chapter?").

Reread all or portions of the text to clarify misunderstandings or extend and deepen understanding. Once students know what they do and do not understand, they can return to the text to reread, their purpose in this case depending on their needs. Those students who have a flawed or incomplete understanding of the text, who cannot answer the PQ fully, should return to find the details related to those parts of the PQ they cannot yet answer. These students need to know how to skim and scan, running their eyes over the page to find just the information they still need; these same students might need additional support through such interventions as reading aloud, thinking aloud, reciprocal teaching, or guided instruction in the use of a new strategy aimed at their particular needs. Other students, such as those who can answer the PQ fully, should reread the text to answer more demanding questions for such sophisticated purposes as stylistic or rhetorical analysis.

Determine what is important to remember and how best to retain that information from the reading. Once students finish reading the text, they need to learn how to select what is important enough to remember for future use when reading, writing, or taking tests. First, students need some sense of criteria for such retention. In this case, what they need to remember depends on how they are likely to use it. Sometimes I ask students to "think like a teacher" (as scary as that is to them!) and generate the kinds of questions or list of subjects teachers would likely include on a test. If someone suggests, for example, "the types of uniforms the soldiers wore during the Civil War," we can have a quick discussion as a class to determine if that is, in fact, relevant to the discussion of the Civil War and, if so, why. If, on the other hand, they are writing a paper in response to the PQ, "Was the Civil War a 'just war'?" this will yield a different crop of questions. Regardless of the task, students need to learn how to figure out what the "take-aways" are so they arrive at the next stage—an exam, a paper, a discussion—ready and able to demonstrate their understanding.

Matt and Josh jot down first impressions of their book prior to participating in a class discussion.

Sometimes this can be accomplished by using something as simple as a scale of one to ten, asking students to score a certain piece of information and explain why they think it is so important that they should remember it. Finally, the question of *how* to remember this information arises, for here students are looking for ways not only to remember these key details but to add them to their background knowledge for future use when reading about related subjects. Which memory strategy is best (mnemonics, cognitive maps, acronyms) depends on the material and students' individual cognitive styles.

Reflect on their process in order to improve their knowledge and application of their process. This step in the reading process is one students will not do on their own; rather, it is something teachers must build into the process, taking the time to have students identify what did and did not work—and why. I have them do this both in writing and through discussion. Sometimes in class I will ask a student who came up with a particularly compelling interpretation, "What questions did you ask to arrive at that idea, Jamil?" If a student has a flawed interpretation, I might ask instead, "Why do you think that, Ana?" In my AP Literature class, students read the weekly poem, a poem I choose, every day at the beginning of class, focusing on some new aspect of the poem each day. Toward the end of the week, as readers are developing a more effective understanding of the poem, I inevitably ask them to identify which of the techniques they used and questions they asked made the biggest difference in advancing their understanding. They write these down in their reader's notebooks, a place where they do their informal thinking about the texts we read.

2. Teach Students to Be Strategic Readers

Conscientious readers are like good drivers who pay attention to all the important signs along the road but disregard distractions that might cost them time or get them lost. When such drivers arrive at their destination, they can remember the key details from the journey and report them in a clear, organized fashion, elaborating, when appropriate, with description and supporting details to capture what the trip was like. In contrast, inattentive readers tend to speed right past the signs, getting lost, or otherwise feeling unsure of their progress, often as a result of being distracted or not knowing which signs are most important to read. If they finally do arrive at their destination, it often seems a fluke. Instead of pleasant stories about how they got there and what happened along the way, they tell of their frustration, time lost, and their intention never to return.

This is all to say that effective readers establish a clear purpose before they begin to read, then evaluate the text as they go, determining which ideas and details are most relevant to that purpose. They make use of a variety of textual features, including such external elements as headings, subheadings, captions, graphics, figures, and fonts, to determine which information is most important. In addition, they draw on their knowledge of text structures—cause and effect, problem and solution, compare and contrast—to identify and understand key details as they read, using these structures as something like a filter to sift the text, the way gold miners sifted the river silt to find the precious nuggets. Like those miners who knew where to look and how to find the gold, smart readers develop the textual intelligence needed to locate and make inferences about the main ideas and how certain details support those ideas.

Before students can identify these ideas, though, they need to prepare themselves, primarily by establishing a purpose for their reading and previewing the text to get some sense of the lay of the land (i.e., how the text is written, organized, designed). After they finish reading, they need some way to assemble those main ideas and supporting details to help them retain and be able to recall them, all of which shows they actually understood what they read. Here are four main guiding principles readers should keep in mind:

Guiding Principles

- Preview the text in light of your purpose.
- Use textual features to determine importance.
- Examine text structures to identify main ideas and supporting details.
- Summarize the text to aid understanding and retention.

Preview the text in light of your purpose.

When talking about main ideas and supporting details, it is useful to distinguish between fiction and informational texts. Fiction offers few of the handrails that support the informational reader: different font sizes and formats, the use of color, captions, easily discernible text structures organized around a main idea that is usually found at the beginning of the paragraph, and all the details in the paragraph organized to support that main idea. Still, it helps to preview literary texts also, as it gives readers a way to gauge the difficulty of language, estimate the length of time required for reading, identify the subject of the chapter or story, and determine the strategies that might best help them identify the key ideas and supporting details. Teachers need to teach students how to do the following when previewing both literary and informational texts:

Identify the subject of the passage, chapter, or article. To do this, show students how to skim the text by looking for key or recurring words, noting headings and subheadings, paying attention to captions or images, and glancing at the first and last lines of the paragraphs in the selection.

Create their own purpose question or use the assigned one to identify the reason for reading. In most content area classes—World History, for example—the purpose is often contained in the chapter itself. That is, students are reading to answer the question the chapter is posing. This question typically lurks beneath the surface of such chapter titles or subheadings as "The Great Depression." Thus the purpose question (PQ) becomes, "What was the Great Depression?" Subsequent readings might organize the passage around more specific questions found in subheadings such as "Causes of the Great Depression." In such cases, the PQ becomes, "What were the causes of the Great Depression?"

Preview any related matter—study questions, captions, headings, bold words, figures, art, or footnotes—that can further prepare readers to identify and understand the main idea and supporting details.

Use their PQ and what they glean in their preview to establish criteria they can use to evaluate the importance of information once they actually begin reading the text. For example, if you are reading an article by a historian about the traits of great leaders across time, you should create a mental filter that sifts out any information unrelated to the question, "What are the qualities of history's great leaders?" While a story about Churchill's learning difficulties as a child may be interesting, it has no apparent relevance to how he led and thus could be screened out; whereas his experience in South Africa early in his career would be relevant and should be read closely.

Consider the text structure as you preview to get a quick sense of how information is organized, so you can orient yourself in terms of where the important information in the text will likely be found and how the text in general will unfold.

Use textual features to determine importance.

In our world of growing media forms and formats, our notion of text—which includes not only traditional printed pages but also e-books, computer screens, and colorful diagrams intermixed with images and words—is quickly evolving. What was once a white page made of paper with black characters inked onto it has morphed into electronic pages, "digital ink," touch-screen multimedia documents with embedded video, and audiobooks heard on iPods without visual text. Yet the more the page changes, the more it remains the same in one important way: every page has a variety of features used to convey information, create order, and signal importance. In textbooks, the word in the bold font, for example, appears as a hotlink when published on a Web page or formatted for the Kindle (an e-book reader developed by Amazon.com). The end result is a text made from different features, all of which have a purpose; such features make the reader a user as much as a reader of texts. If students are to be able to navigate their way through a text and identify the main idea and supporting details, they will need to know what these features are and how to make sense of them along the way. Here are some ideas to help them:

Identify for students the key features—bold words, headers, subheadings, spatial arrangement, captions, font size, etc.—that signal importance as main ideas and supporting details in the larger text or within the paragraph.

Display a sample of the text—from a textbook, Web site, or map—via a document camera, overhead, or LCD projector, and give students a tour of the features, identifying each one and explaining how it signals importance or indicates where you can find more information about a given detail. For example, in textbooks, bold words often indicate that definitions for that word are located in the glossary; other books use symbols to direct students to margins for notes or definitions.

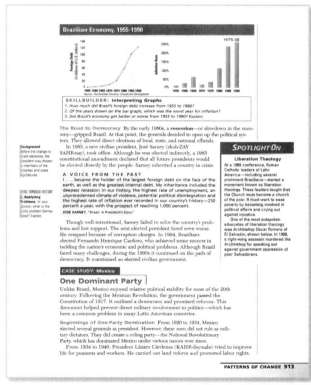

I photocopy sample textbook pages like this one onto a transparency or project them using an LCD, then circle and underline key features as I explain them.

Ask students to create a brief outline based on textual features to indicate order of importance. This generally works only with textbook pages where the font sizes and other features, such as color, indicate importance and relationship. Such analysis would make most sense when introducing a complex new text, for instance earlier in the year when students receive new textbooks.

As a class, generate a key to the text features, posting it on the wall and adding to it as you go. These features would indicate not only what is important but what is *not* important as it relates to the main and supporting ideas. In math and science textbooks, for example, publishers often put icons in the margins around problems or written passages. It turns out these are often there merely to suggest school-to-career links; that is, an icon with a microscope next to a passage suggests that those in the science field need to know and often use this type of equation. Thus the icon is not helpful in indicating main ideas or supporting details.

Examine text structures to identify main ideas and supporting details.

Text structures refer to the way information is organized in a piece of writing, particularly a paragraph, which comes in several types and can be organized to achieve different ends. Fiction paragraphs are usually either narrative in form, telling a story, or descriptive. Two other types, expository and persuasive, are common in informational texts designed to explain a topic or convince the reader. Aside from the type of paragraph, writers can arrange the ideas, both main and supporting, within the paragraph in different ways, depending on their purpose. Readers who know and can recognize these different types of paragraphs and organizational structures are better prepared to find the main ideas and supporting details because they know how the text functions and where information is likely to be placed to achieve the intended effect. These patterns are briefly described below.

Text Structures

Chronological
Information is arranged by time; typically used in narrative texts.

Spatial (or Geographic)
Details are organized by location; used frequently when describing.

Compare–Contrast
Information is organized to show how certain subjects are similar and different; used in a variety of types of paragraphs and for a range of purposes.

Problem–Solution
Details about a problem are clearly outlined, then followed by the solution; used for different purposes, but especially to persuade.

Cause–Effect
Information about the causes (e.g., of global warming) are discussed, followed by the effects; used in different types of writing and for several different purposes.

List
Details are presented one sentence after another, with no discernible order, suggesting all are equally important; often used to describe or inform.

Order of Importance
Information appears according to some ranking principle (e.g., from least to most important, or most to least important); applied by writers attempting to explain, persuade, or describe.

You can teach students how to apply these structures to identify key and supporting information through a range of techniques:

Provide direct instruction to students about these different text structures, even in more advanced-level classes where students often encounter more dense academic prose.

Ask students to color code or label (e.g., "MI" for main idea, "SD" for supporting detail) contents according to their function or importance. When doing this, you should always model to provide a more concrete illustration of the ideas you are trying to teach them.

Display sample passages, using both numbers and visual arrangement (e.g., in outline format) to show where the main idea is and how the supporting details are placed in relation to the main idea throughout the text. For example, using a passage I can quickly type or copy from a Web site and, formatting it as described, I project it from my laptop via the LCD projector while I verbally annotate it for the class. If, for example, we are working on how to compare and contrast, I will bring in samples from the texts we are studying or the textbook we already use. Either way, both color and spatial arrangement prove tremendously helpful in showing students how to find and make sense of the main idea and supporting details.

Ask students to use graphic organizers or structured notes when reading a particular article; these organizers or notes should correspond with the text structure of the assigned reading. In my freshman English class, for example, in August they read a series of articles on success. I give them a structured note-tracking sheet I created to help them identify the main idea and organize the supporting details. This sheet resembles a spreadsheet and is designed to capture the key ideas in the order they appear.

Dylan uses a graphic organizer to help him examine the structure of the text and prepare to write about it.

Teach students to annotate the text based on its organizational pattern. When reading an article about Abraham Lincoln and why he was a successful leader, for example, students identified the main trait described in each paragraph that led to his success as president and recorded them in the margin. Next, they underlined the supporting details in the paragraph that related to that main idea. As an alternative to drawing arrows, try highlighting or labeling the supporting details that relate to the main idea you write in the margin.

Summarize the text to aid understanding and retention.

To write a summary, students must know the subject, what the author says about it (main idea), and how the author develops the main idea (supporting details). Summaries can also come in different forms: oral, written, or visual. Whatever form you use, the basics remain the same: an effective summary clearly indicates the subject and the main idea about that subject, and includes those details that support the main idea. Students are not always ready to go straight from reading to summarizing, however; they often need help preparing to write such summaries. This means giving students either a structured note-taking technique or a graphic organizer that will help them extract and organize the main and supporting ideas. Here are some specific instructional techniques you might consider:

Ask students to make a list of the most important ideas after they finish reading the assigned text. I often make this more specific, depending on the type of text, by saying, "List the five most important details from this article." After discussing why students think these are the most important, we consider the criteria they used to make their selection. In preparation for writing their summaries, we create agreed-upon criteria that they apply to their list to winnow it down. Having identified the most important ideas, I then redirect them back to the text to find the relevant details that support that main idea and ask them to add these to their notes. At that point, they are ready to write their summaries. Depending on the class or the difficulty of the text, I may provide a sample summary or model how I might begin one, usually

Mark and Samantha add their own ideas to the list of key ideas from an article they read in Senior English.

doing this on my computer and displaying it on the screen via the LCD projector.

Ask students to use graphic organizers or other strategies, such as concept maps, that are designed to help them identify the main idea and supporting details. While not often necessary for advanced students, such structured and visual pre-writing and note-taking methods help students sort out their ideas and get them better organized prior to writing. When using such techniques, I demonstrate this on the overhead to facilitate or give students examples to follow so they know what to do. When students finish, they have well-organized notes they can use to write an effective summary.

Identify for students the elements and qualities of an effective summary, providing examples to illustrate what you say. Some go so far as to give students a rubric with a checklist of descriptors students can be sure to include in their summary. (See the chart on next page.)

When writing a summary, try to use some of these "summarizing" verbs to indicate the author's thinking:

argues	describes	implies
asserts	discusses	insists
compares	emphasizes	mentions
concludes	examines	notes
considers	explores	points out
contends	focuses on	states
contrasts	illustrates	suggests

Guidelines for Creating an Effective Summary

BEFORE READING

1. Establish your purpose.
2. Skim the document.
3. Choose a note-taking method.

DURING READING

4. Take notes to help you answer these questions:
   - Who or what is the main subject?
   - What are the most important events, ideas, or people?
   - What are the main causes or effects?
5. Develop criteria to clarify what is important enough to include in your summary.
6. Evaluate information as you read to determine if you should include it in your notes.

AFTER READING

7. Write your summary, which should be organized as follows:
   - The length should be considerably shorter than the original article (e.g., not longer than a page).
   - Identify the title, author, and topic in the first sentence.
   - State the main idea in the second sentence.
   - Include three to five sentences in which you explain—in your own words—what the author is saying about the subject.
   - Include one or two interesting quotations, examples, or details.
   - Retain the author's original meaning.
   - Arrange the ideas in the order in which they appear in the article.
   - Include transitions, such as *according to* and the author's name, to show that you are summarizing someone else's ideas.
   - Use enough information from the article that someone who has not read the article will understand the ideas.

I sometimes write a sample introduction myself or use one I copied from a former student, projecting it from the overhead so I can annotate what I did and how it corresponds with the guidelines. Here is a sample summary I wrote for my freshman English class:

In "Miraculous Survivors: Why They Live While Others Die," John Blake examines who survives during terrible events and what they have in common. While each person is different, he argues that there are traits that allow these people to overcome their circumstances. More than anything else, Blake emphasizes the important role that mental strength plays. Survivors are "not whiners," and tend to be "independent thinkers," which prevents them from falling into the traps that others often do. In addition to these mental traits, survivors also establish a goal and use it to keep them focused on the future and their return instead of on the crisis at hand. Some concentrate on seeing their family, while others feed on their anger, driven by the desire to confront the people responsible for their troubles. Finally, those who survive show a willingness to do whatever it takes to survive, even if it means wrapping themselves up in seaweed to stay warm or living off of urine and paper until they are rescued. What unites them all, Blake implies, is a "will to live" and the belief, often expressed through prayer, that they will make it home to those they love and continue on with their lives.

Deliver oral summaries in teacher-student conferences, through brief presentations, or during class discussions. These follow roughly the same pattern as the written summary but provide a useful alternative that strives to reach the same end: teaching students to identify the main idea and supporting details, then communicate these—in this case, orally—in order to demonstrate understanding of the material they read.

Create a graphic or visual summary of the material.

This serves the same purposes outlined above, but does so using a more visual means. This graph, chart, diagram, map, or other visual explanation could be included as part of an oral presentation, though this is optional. In a health class, for example, the teacher might ask students to produce a visual summary of the chapter examining the effects of fast food on the body and mind over time; the economics teacher might ask students to summarize the chapter about supply and demand using graphs that identify the main idea in a header and use the graph to illustrate the supporting details.

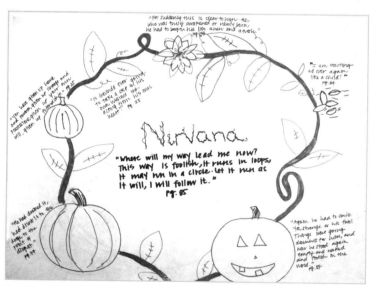

Students created this visual summary of the stages the main character goes through on his journey in Hermann Hesse's novel *Siddhartha*.

3. Use Background Knowledge and Make Connections

In his wonderful DVD *The Power of Art*, historian Simon Schama looks at the same painting I do—Caravaggio's *David With the Head of Goliath*—and sees things I cannot. Where I see only the familiar biblical story of David and Goliath, Schama sees a young, innocent Caravaggio looking on in disgust at the head of Goliath painted to resemble the depraved criminal Caravaggio had become by the end of his life. What allows Schama to see what I cannot, to understand something about the painting that is not available to me? It is his background knowledge—about Italian painting during the Baroque period, about Caravaggio himself, about the Bible and that historical period in general. Like a reader making sense of a difficult, unfamiliar text, I *look* at the painting but cannot make sense of it. If we could scan Schama's head as he looked at the painting, it would light up like a Christmas tree, signaling connections to the different areas of his knowledge and experience; my brain scan, in contrast, would resemble the Great Plains in the middle of the night: here and there an isolated point of light indicating

Guiding Principles

- **Build and teach students how to access their prior knowledge before they read.**

- **Enhance and apply background knowledge while they read.**

- **Organize, store, and use prior knowledge afterwards to understand and remember what they read.**

Emilie and her classmates use visual metaphors to build background knowledge about war prior to reading a story by Tim O'Brien.

remote, unconnected outposts, each burning a lone candle about to be blown out by the winds of my own ignorance.

Background knowledge is arguably the most important component of successful reading; the ability to access, build on, and apply it when reading is crucial to one's success with new and difficult material. Imagine the difference in comprehension between the highest- and lowest-performing readers in your class according to the Gates-MacGinitie reading test. John reads at a fourth-grade level; Mike, who sits next to the underachieving reader, scores at the post-high school level. One would assume the results would be predictable when these students are asked to read a very demanding article in which the author uses detailed data to analyze two baseball teams that will play in the World Series and explain why one will beat the other. But a curious thing happens: When tested on the material, John, the "struggling" reader, dramatically outperforms Mike, whose Gates scores suggest he is ready for Harvard. How to explain the discrepancy? Background knowledge. The text, like so many types of texts in different content areas, is laden with specialized terms, allusions, data, historical references, and names of players, positions, and techniques, about which John knows everything and Mike knows little or nothing. Thus Mike cannot get a foothold on the text, can't climb into it because he has no prior experience with such texts and lacks any means of making connections that would allow him to understand what he reads.

Background knowledge, however, means more than knowing who Goliath was and why David killed him. It includes having some knowledge about the following topics and issues:

authors	concepts	subject matter
events	conventions	text features
genres	cultural literacy	text types
history	other fields	vocabulary
cultures	people	stories/myth

Such knowledge is often subject to the biases that come from previous experiences, personal values, and lessons. So while prior knowledge is essential, it is also potentially flawed as a result of incorrect or incomplete knowledge which, when combined with students' possible biases, can profoundly shape their interpretation of a text. When thinking about background knowledge, we might compare it to our computers and how the information is arranged into folders. If you are about to investigate the subject of war, you might click on the folder labeled *War* to see what you have in there. For some, it will be empty; they have no experience with or knowledge about the subject. Others, however, will have stashed random unorganized documents, while still others will have carefully organized subfolders, with labels such as *Vietnam*, *World War Two*, *Iraq War*, and so on. When these people go to access this prior knowledge, it will be organized and therefore useful in helping them understand and store new information about the same subject. Background knowledge needs to be organized in ways that allow us to find and use it; moreover, as we *add* to our store of knowledge through continued studies, we must store that new information in logical ways that reinforce existing connections and help to develop new ones about that subject for potential use in the future.

Build and teach students to access their prior knowledge before they read.

Background knowledge plays an essential role throughout the reading process, not just before we begin reading. What's more, it refers not only to what we already know but also to what we need to know to complete the assigned reading task successfully. Here, however, we focus on what to do before reading, an action some (Wilhelm 2001) call "frontloading." As we do before leaving on a trip, we gather knowledge—consulting maps, guidebooks, and Web sites to learn something about the place we are going so, once we arrive, we will know how to find our way around and understand what we see. Some (Jensen 2005; Willis 2006) refer to such frontloading as "priming the pump," which means getting the brain ready to learn new information by activating the neural networks of existing knowledge about the subject we are about to study. Yet it is not always a subject we need to learn more about before reading; oftentimes it is the genre or certain features of a given text we need to know more about if we are to read it well. Thus as teachers we need to also evaluate, prior to reading, what our students already know and need to learn, for example, about sonnets or fables, Web sites or persuasive essays, so we can provide the necessary background knowledge that will ensure their success. During this phase, we should also monitor—and teach students to monitor—the accuracy and biases of their background knowledge, as students often have preexisting notions of what is true about a subject, the world, or people. Finally, such pre-reading work, particularly with background knowledge, increases engagement in the text at hand as it helps students connect what they know and consider their own interests, inspiring them to learn more about the text. You can ignite interest and help students access their background knowledge through the following techniques:

Generate questions, brainstorm associations, and make predictions based on the title or topic. You can have students do these on their own or in groups. In addition, ask students to make connections between the assigned text and previous studies, the world, and their own experiences. Judith Langer (1981) developed a more formal process for such generating; her PreP method asks teachers and students to:

- Examine the text for key terms and concepts they need to know.

- Brainstorm associations students might have with the topic (e.g., write "Revolution" on the board and jot down anything that comes to students' minds about this topic).

- Reflect on these connections and associations, asking such questions as, "How is this idea related to the subject we are studying or the text we are about to read?" "Why does this idea come to mind when I think about this subject?"

- Refine and revise ideas as students prepare to begin reading, asking such questions as, "What new information can we add to our initial associations with this subject?" "What more specific connections can we make between what we know about this topic and the text we are about to read?"

- Evaluate what students currently know about a topic or text before beginning to read. This can be done through formal means, such as pretests and anticipation guides, or via more informal methods, such as class discussions and written responses to specific questions. During such discussions, be prepared to challenge their thinking, asking them such questions as, "Why do you think that?" and "How do you know that?" Much of what students think they know is based on speculation or hearsay, biased by their own experiences or perspectives. For example, a discussion about Arthur Miller's *The Crucible* might involve asking students what they know about both the Salem witchcraft trials and the McCarthy era, both of which are central to the play's themes. Student responses might be colored by their incomplete knowledge or experiences with communism or a culture they may have grown up in prior to coming to the United States.

Identify and anticipate gaps or flaws in students' knowledge about a subject or type of text prior to reading. When teaching a particular type of literature, a play like Miller's *The Crucible*, for example, there are dramatic conventions they must know but may not. Identifying these gaps or anticipating them (by asking teachers from the previous year if they taught their students about tragedy, for instance) allows you to address them through direct instruction in or supplemental readings about that subject.

Provide students necessary background information about an author, text, or subject prior to reading about it. You can provide such information through a variety of means, including lecture, supplemental readings, videos that contain the relevant details, investigations online, discussions, or guest speakers. Prior to reading Elie Wiesel's memoir *Night*, for example, in which he details his experiences as a child during the Holocaust, I took my freshman students to the computer lab where they used the National Holocaust Memorial Museum Web site to answer certain key questions about the Holocaust. They used information from that initial inquiry to formulate questions for a guest speaker who came the next day to discuss her experiences during the Holocaust, all of which provided students with the background knowledge they needed to understand Wiesel's memoir.

Make connections between the subject students are reading and their own experiences, knowledge, and the world. Such connections serve to generate curiosity and increase the likelihood of students being more engaged when they read, since they now see some ways in which reading relates to their own interests and experiences. For example, prior to reading *Antigone*, my seniors write about a time when they or someone they know took a stand, even if it came at some cost; they can look to historical figures they respect, people such as Rosa Parks, or their own experience of perhaps protesting an issue at a local political rally. Because I want them to focus on what the play says about law,

Daniel and Harrison make connections between *Antigone*, their own experiences, and those of historical figures such as Rosa Parks.

they read a page with ten different quotations—from such prominent people as George Bernard Shaw and Oliver Wendell Holmes—about some aspect of the law. Students choose one from the list and explain what it means and respond to it based on their own ideas or experience. We then use these as the basis for a class discussion before they go home to begin reading Sophocles' play.

Create posters, bookmarks, handouts, graphic organizers, or other materials that include key information or reminders you want students to have available as they read. A social studies teacher might, for example, create a graphic organizer that lists certain Constitutional amendments in one column and provides space in another for them to make notes about each amendment.

Katy and Melissa use graphic organizers to help them identify and examine the relationship between key ideas in two texts they read.

Prior to reading the text, students may have learned about these amendments; in order to reinforce that learning and extend it through application, they are to take notes, capturing specific details related to each amendment.

Enhance and apply background knowledge while they read.

Background knowledge also plays a vital role during the reading process. While we read, we are constantly drawing on what we know to comprehend what we do not; we routinely encounter material we do not understand and so must stop to build up our background knowledge—through supplemental reading, a lecture, or film—so we can complete the reading assignment. In such cases it's a bit like running out of gas and getting stuck on the side of the road; after filling the tank you can continue on your way. During the reading process, we are trying not only to understand but also to travel deeper into the text and its ideas. New ideas arise, unexpected twists in the plot occur (if we are reading fiction), unfamiliar terrain appears suddenly (in the form of textual features, genre conventions, and specialized vocabulary), all of which can confuse us and undermine our ability to reach our destination: comprehension. Again, comprehension is fundamental but it is not the only goal, for if students cannot drill down to the bigger ideas, if they can do no more than say what the author said, they are trapped at the surface level, unable to apply what they are learning to the larger purpose of the class. The student who can summarize the Emancipation Proclamation but not apply its ideas to American history or analyze how it shaped that history is not the competent reader society and the workplace require. The following five techniques offer guidance in how to address the role of background knowledge during the process of reading any assigned text in the content areas:

Monitor and evaluate students' comprehension as they read through discussion, written responses, or formative assessments designed to assess their understanding of key concepts. Misreadings sometimes arise during the reading process as a result of inaccurate or incomplete knowledge that undermines comprehension. To return to an earlier analogy, these moments of confusion compare to the moment a traveler realizes he is lost and must pull over to the side of the road. While it is important for teachers to identify and anticipate when such trouble occurs and then work to resolve it, it is ultimately a skill students must develop in themselves if they are to become independent, fluent readers. One way to evaluate such comprehension, aside from those listed above, is to use what some call "exit cards." Have students write on an index card the answer to a few well-phrased questions that would indicate their degree of understanding. In a health class, for example, the teacher might ask students to jot down the three key ideas from an article about the relationship between junk food, brain development, and diabetes. Students' responses on these cards would help the teacher know if she needed to pull back and address key

Dom highlights those parts of the text he does not understand prior to discussing them in a group with his fellow students.

background information related to the subject of junk food, brain development, or diabetes. On other occasions, when the text is particularly challenging, I ask students to highlight or underline what they do not understand as they read; we then pause to discuss, as a class or in small groups, the parts they do *not* understand; this is helpful with all students, but I find it especially useful with more advanced students who often feel pressured to pretend they get it all; this gives them permission to acknowledge they do not.

Supplement understanding and repair confusion or comprehension throughout the reading process. When students understand the material at the surface level, it is often best to build on that by supplementing the reading, even if it means interrupting the larger assignment to read something smaller. In my senior English class, for example, students reading *Antigone* and *Oedipus Rex* examine the role and concept of law (among other subjects) in the two plays. As we read through each play, I provide concise readings about law to get them to think in new ways once it is clear they have a grasp of the play's basic ideas. First, I ask them to read a short parable about law written by Kafka; then I give them a short newspaper article about evolving conceptions of law; finally, a few days later, I arrange for a lawyer to come in and talk to them about law—what it is, how it works, and how it relates to the play.

A local lawyer visits our class to help us understand law and how it relates to the story we are reading.

When they stumble on concepts like "higher law" or "supernatural law," which Antigone discusses in the play, I have them read excerpts from Thoreau's essay on that subject.

In my freshman English class, students need help figuring out how to understand discussion of the "Troubles" in Ireland during the 1970s. Here my concern is more with repairing their confusion about the basic ideas so they can get an initial understanding of the story "The Sniper." Some don't know what a civil war is; others stumble on terms like "republic." We pause to read a short article in the textbook titled, "Children of the Troubles," that explains what the "Troubles" were, how they affected Ireland's children, and what a group called Project Children did to help them heal from the emotional crises brought on by a civil war. I supplement this with a short video on YouTube that gives us a tour of the Civil War through the remarkable murals that appear throughout Ireland, especially Northern Ireland. Then, after discussing these—what they mean and how they relate to the story— my students resume reading with a better grasp of the

Here I use images from Google to illustrate
a text reference.

situation. During the reading process we sometimes need
to supplement the reading or deepen their understanding
of the text; this is best done through readings, short video
clips, experts, webquests, lecture, or discussion.

**Generate connections and questions throughout the
reading process.** To read is to inquire; thus questions are
a natural and important part of our reading process. So,
too, are connections. We make them intuitively as we
read, using our experience in church or in the forest to
consider how it is similar to or different from that of the
character in the story, or wondering how the information
we learn in health or history relates to the character
in the book we are reading in English. Teachers can
use a range of techniques to help students make these
connections. They can use sentence prompts like these:

> _____ is similar to _____ in this story in
> that both characters _____.

> Although both were charismatic, innovative leaders,
> Lincoln faced different challenges than Washington did
> during the Revolution: Washington _____, while
> Lincoln _____.

Another approach is to create graphic organizers or structured note-taking sheets to use while students read. My freshman English students, who read a collection of stories, essays, and poems as part of a unit on survival, use a structured note-taking sheet I created to identify the key elements of survival and to gather examples from the story as they read.

Trait/ Description	Example from Text (w/pg #)	Explanation (how this contributes to survival)
Courage Overcome fears to do what you didn't think you could	"Then, in necessity and tenderness, she swiftly did what had to be done" (18). "She felt a sense of response, of obligation . . ." (18).	Nora's courage allows her to overcome her own fears and anxieties about cutting off Pleny's finger; she finds in herself the courage to do "what had to be done" if he was to live and she was to survive living out in the remote world of the plains.

Another technique to consider is coding or annotating the text. Prior to reading the text, you may have talked to students about a specific concept or aspect of the text. This approach forces students to read more closely, using their background knowledge during the reading process to evaluate key details and determine if they accord with some idea. In a developmental reading class, for example, I ask students to study the elements of successful people as defined by a variety of sources. As they read an article about Dr. Benjamin Carson, an African-American neurosurgeon who was the first to separate twins joined at the head, they must label each element (e.g., determination, courage) they think contributes to his success. One final method to consider involves revisiting and monitoring predictions the students may have made before reading the text. Prior to reading, teachers often ask students to draw on their background knowledge and, using the title and the subject of the text as a guide, make a prediction; at specific junctures throughout the reading, students should stop to evaluate the accuracy of their predictions, revising them if necessary in light of new information that leads to new insights.

Throughout the reading process, provide support to all students who may be struggling. Some of your English Language Learners may be having a difficult time with unfamiliar vocabulary, complex sentence structures, or unfamiliar concepts. Others may not yet know how to read a particular type of text or how to read the way you asked them to (e.g., "analyze the author's style or arguments as you read"). Any challenge requires your support; otherwise your students may disengage, not complete or understand the assigned reading, and, ultimately, fail. Several techniques come to mind that you can use to help them build or activate the necessary background knowledge, several of which have been mentioned above. One of the best is reading aloud and, as you do, thinking aloud. Sometimes students don't know how a text sounds, where to place the emphasis, or how it should be read. This is particularly common when reading speeches, poems, or plays. If I notice that students are not understanding what they read, I stop them and ask, "What seems to be the problem?" They might say they do not understand what the author is talking about because, for example, they don't know what the Spanish words mean in Rudolfo Anaya's novel *Bless Me, Ultima*, or they are puzzling over his reference to an *adobe house* since they have never been to the Southwest. To support them, I read selected passages aloud, choosing those with Spanish; as I read, I interrupt myself to explain (think aloud) how I make sense of these Spanish words and sentences using context clues from the story. To address those details foreign to students—adobe houses, *curanderas*, dust devils—I pull up Google Images on my classroom computer and switch on the LCD projector. I display images of adobe houses or *curanderas* (women with knowledge about plants and herbs that can be used to heal) and discuss what students are seeing and how these images relate to the story. Using visuals to build background knowledge dispels confusion and makes for a lively discussion as we consider which of the twelve photos of a *curandera* most closely resembles the description of Ultima in the novel.

Reflect on the process and strategies students are using to evaluate their effectiveness and determine if other approaches would be more appropriate. Also, students should reflect on what they still need to learn and how best they might achieve that goal. It is important to interrupt students' reading process sometimes, asking them to hit the pause button for a few minutes while they think about what they know and need to know. One way to facilitate such reflection is to ask them to draw two columns, heading one "What I Know" and the other, "What I Need to Know." While they read, students need to monitor not only their processes but also their knowledge, paying attention to what works and why so they can adjust their process as needed or ask for help.

Organize, store, and use prior knowledge afterwards to understand and remember what they read.

Several processes involve prior knowledge after we read. First, we draw on all we know now from the story (as well as our own experience and knowledge of the world and other texts, some of which may be written by the same author) to arrive at some conclusions about what the story means. Then, if we are effective readers, we decide what information from this text, and the experience of reading it, might serve us in the future and label and store it in ways that facilitate retention and eventual recall. If you are working with shorter texts or difficult material, it is always a good idea to reread the text, as this affords a deeper understanding in general and a finer appreciation of, for example, the author's style. Finally, once we finish reading the story, we are able to make connections between what we knew before and what we have learned by reading this text, adding to our knowledge base—not only of this text but of this type of text. The following suggestions all help to make the best use of background knowledge *after* students finish their initial or final reading of a text:

Evaluate students' understanding about the subject, genre, or author. At the beginning, and throughout the process, students have made various predictions based on what they thought was true; having completed the text, however, they may now realize their knowledge was obsolete, biased, or otherwise flawed. One way to do this, if you happened to use the KWL organizer (see pages 76–78 for more information on this technique), is to complete that last column on the organizer—*What I Learned*—and compare that with what students wrote in the first two columns—what they (thought they) *knew* and what they *wanted* to know. This is a crucial phase of the reading and learning process, for it is here that old knowledge is updated with new, more accurate knowledge that can be drawn upon as background knowledge on subsequent reading tasks in this class or others.

Organize, connect, and integrate this new knowledge into the existing network of knowledge about the world, this author, this subject, or this type of text. One way to do this is through writing, whether in the informal context of a written response in a notebook or the more structured form of an essay. Other possible avenues to explore would include graphic organizers designed to synthesize new and old information about the subject and, in the process, identify existing categories into which the new knowledge can be organized for later recall. Some of this material can also be integrated through facilitated discussion in groups or as a class. A history teacher, for example, who has just assigned an article about the Gulf War can ask students to compare how it is similar to or different from the Vietnam or Iraq wars—which students may know through family experience, news coverage, or films. As she facilitates the discussion, the teacher can list on the board categories and connections as a way of reinforcing and connecting new knowledge. In this respect, such new knowledge becomes prior knowledge when, in subsequent days or months, students read about other subjects, some of which may not be familiar, and so the cycle continues.

Transform new knowledge into artifacts to improve understanding and increase retention of material for future use as prior knowledge. When students take new knowledge and integrate that with existing knowledge, it becomes part of their long-term memory and can be drawn on—think of it as an intellectual bank account to which they make deposits and, when using prior knowledge, make withdrawals—when reading subsequent new or related texts. Such knowledge can be transformed into plays, news scripts to be performed for the class, posters, discussions, debates, graphs, charts, maps, and written works such as articles or essays. In my freshman English class, where approximately 95 percent of the students (I surveyed the class!) play video games regularly, I allowed students to create a video game (on paper, with directions) based on the short story, "The Most Dangerous Game." This is a complex story, the longest of the bunch that we read; it's also filled with details that draw on their prior knowledge of plot and setting as well as video games in which one has to overcome a range of obstacles to achieve an objective.

Confirm and revise predictions and elaborate on this new learning to further reinforce and improve retention of the knowledge. In addition to predictions, students will have made inferences and drawn conclusions, both of which rely heavily on prior knowledge to complete. Now is the time to revisit the basis of these predictions, inferences, and conclusions to revise or retire such prior knowledge if it was flawed in some way. As important as confirming and reinforcing these predictions and conclusions, students must elaborate on their thinking through writing or discussion. For example, students in my freshman English class, after reading the short story "Plainswoman," use a Venn diagram to take notes as they read "The Necklace," so they can make connections between the two stories and draw conclusions about how the two women survived their different but related ordeals. They use the Venn diagram as the basis for a writing assignment that asks them to compare and contrast the two women, drawing specific examples from the stories to support and illustrate their ideas. My instructional goal here is, of course, to improve their comprehension of the stories, but it is also to ensure that students remember some of the key concepts related to survival as these two stories are part of a much larger unit on survival. Thus the writing and subsequent discussion, both of which help develop students' writing and oral skills, help solidify the background knowledge garnered from these two stories so they can draw on it not only when they read the next article, poem, or story, but also when they write their final paper about the overall question, "What does it take to be a survivor?"

Reflect on what they learned and how they learned it, focusing also on what they did to remember it. A rich knowledge base, one that works like a well-stocked ATM that allows us to make as many withdrawals as we need (so long as we keep making new deposits of equal or greater amounts), requires maintenance as well as a keen understanding of how our own individual brain works best. How do we remember and make the best use of the knowledge and experience we have to connect seemingly unrelated ideas encountered across different texts? In my class, this process may be as simple and quick as asking my students to write in their notebooks what they think is most important to remember from this subject and how it relates to what they already know so they can access it again in the future. Sometimes we know, as in the case of my survival unit, that this new knowledge will be needed within days; in such cases, we can tell students this, asking them to reflect on what is most important to remember and how they can remember it in the days to come. In a recent class, such a discussion led to the suggestion from some students that I create a handout with all the words we had learned for writing about a character. This led to the handout on the next two pages.

Language of Literature: Character

Directions: Use the following word lists to improve your sentence fluency through precise, active words specifically related to writing about and discussing characterization.

Example: Conrad defines Marlowe early on through his observations not his actions, using Marlow as a credible witness to express Conrad's own criticisms of the sins of the European powers in Africa.

NOUNS

action(s)	description	insight	reference
adjective	desire	intention(s)	relationship
allusion	despair	interactions	reliability
antagonist	destiny	interior	reputation
archetype	development	knowledge	role
argument	device	limit(ations)	satire
aspects	dialogue	manners	senses
attire	diction	melancholy	sensibility
attitude	economy	mind	skepticism
attribute	emotions	monologue	soliloquy
behavior	environment	motif	source
capacity	epitome	motivation	spectator
caricature	essence	motive(s)	speech
choice	ethos	movement(s)	stereotype
concern(s)	experience	narrator	struggle(s)
conflict	expression	object	study
contradiction	factors	observations	style
contrast	fate	observer	symbol
convention	feelings	paradox	technique
conversation	foil	parody	theme
conviction	hero/heroine	personality	tone
credibility	idiosyncracies	philosophy	traits
criticisms	illusion	plot	type
definition	implication	position	values
depiction	individual	presence	verisimilitude
depth	inquiry	reason	will

VERBS

animate	construct	describe	emphasize
argue	contradict	desire	epitomize
attribute	contrast	details	establishes
capture	contribute	develop	evoke
cause	converse	discover	expect
choose	declare	distinguish	explore
compare	define	distract	expose
conclude	demonstrate	elaborate	express
confirm	deny	elevate	face
confound	derive	empathize	favor

VERBS (continued)

force	invent	process	shape
illuminate	investigate	prolong	show
illustrate	measure	provide	state
impose	move	react	struggle
indicate	observe	reduce	suggest
infer	occupy	reflects	surmise
influence	offer	refuse	sympathize
inform	poetry	remain	talk
infuse	posit	render	think
inhibit	position	reply	transform
inspire	possess	represents	undergo
instill	present	reveal	witness

ADJECTIVES

absurd	developed	intelligent	realistic
aggressive	devious	interior	reckless
ambitious	devoted	ironic	relevant
amorous	dishonest	irrepressible	round
animated	distinct	irritable	scrupulous
anxious	distinctive	loquacious	secondary
archetypal	dramatic	major	self-absorbed
argumentative	easygoing	manipulative	self-involved
arrogant	elegant	mature	sloppy
awkward	elevated	mendacious	solid
benign	eloquent	minor	spiritual
bitter	enigmatic	moral	spontaneous
bored	envious	mundane	stereotypical
capable	essential	naïve	stock
careless	exacting	nervous	stylish
cautious	exaggerated	noble	subordinate
central	experienced	observant	subtle
churlish	external	omniscient	surface
comic	fictional	outgoing	talkative
compassionate	flamboyant	patient	testy
compatible	formal	pedantic	thin
compelling	fragile	physical	transparent
conniving	frantic	picky	ubiquitous
conscientious	free	plausible	understated
conscious	garrulous	predictable	uninvolved
consistent	gregarious	primary	upright
curious	idiosyncratic	private	verbal
deceitful	independent	proper	vibrant
deep	indirect	provincial	vindictive
demure	inherent	provocative	welcoming
destructive	inner	public	wise
detailed	intellectual	real	worried

4. Ask Questions to Improve and Deepen Comprehension

No tool on the reader's tool belt works as hard as or proves more useful than the question. We use questions to comprehend and clarify the meaning of a text and to extend and connect our understanding to other texts as well as the world outside the texts we read. Reading like doctors (instead of judges), we use questions like stethoscopes to evaluate and monitor the information in and our understanding of the texts, tapping here and there as the doctor does to determine the health of our evolving interpretation. At the heart of a good question is that notion of the *quest*, a purpose one is seeking to fulfill, a learning goal the reader wants to achieve, for as teachers we know that all learning begins with a question. It is this sense of purpose that characterizes the effective, engaged reader and that students must learn to develop within themselves. Yet such habits of mind require direct instruction and guidance, frequent modeling, and regular practice in a variety of circumstances and on a range of texts if students are to internalize these questions. To that end, we must teach students not only which questions to ask but also how and when to ask them. Some questions are more appropriate for literary texts, while others are best used to comprehend informational or nonfiction texts; several strategies focus on comprehending a text, while others (e.g., Question the Author) show students how to seek out and understand the underlying ideas and techniques used to advance those ideas. When teaching students to develop and ask questions, consider the following key ideas, adapting them as needed to meet the needs of your students and curriculum.

Guiding Principles

- Develop students' ability to generate and choose effective questions.

- Teach students to ask a range of questions for different purposes.

- Ask students questions throughout the reading process.

- Teach specific question strategies.

Develop students' ability to generate and choose effective questions.

When we are kids, we ask questions about everything. It's an innate curiosity best represented by such questions as, "Why is the sky blue?" Everything fascinates us, makes us want to know more. As we grow older, though, we encounter material that resists our understanding, leaving us to ask questions more out of frustration such as "Why the heck do we need to know this anyway?" and "What is this about?" Though we can give our students the questions to ask or use the questions waiting at the end of a chapter or story, our greater aim must be to teach them to generate their own questions and select from these questions the most useful few. The following strategies consistently yield not just good questions but the capacity to create and use such questions independently:

> **Ask students to pause before they read and generate two to three questions about the subject and title of the article. Then use these questions to teach them the importance of accessing background knowledge.** Whether they actually respond to the questions depends on your instructional goals. Regardless of whether they answer them, you can extend this activity by herding students into groups and telling them to pool their questions, evaluating and choosing the two most

effective questions. After this, have students report out to the class, during which time you write the questions on the board and ask students what makes these effective questions and how they might respond to them. The objective is not the questions—though they are, of course, useful—but the knowledge of what makes a useful question and how to phrase and use one.

Write on the board or overhead, "Qs to Ask" as a header before reading a type of text or text about a particular topic. Though this is a fine way to access background knowledge (e.g., Qs to Ask About the Civil Rights Movement), I also use it to focus on the questions students should learn to ask about a particular type of text (e.g., Qs to Ask About Poems, Qs to Ask About Fiction). By doing this, I model for my students the habit of mind for engaged learners, reminding them that effective readers pose questions throughout the process, asking about both form and function, both content and concepts. Such questions are best asked *before* students begin reading, as they focus the students, giving them a purpose or a lens through which they can become more critical readers.

- What is F. P. like?
- When does she change?
- Why does she change?
- How does she change?
- Which changes are most important?

Give students sticky notes before they read and ask them to write questions on them. These questions might refer to passages they did not understand, in which case students can stick the note next to the elusive passage, or their questions could be in response to the whole text. When I have students generate questions about the text as a whole, I might have them bring these up to the front and post them on the board, sometimes as a big brainstorm, other times in categories such as "Questions About Characters," "Questions About Themes," and so on. We then use these questions as the basis for our subsequent group or class discussions of the text.

Kevin puts up sticky notes on the timeline. The note above the line identifies what happened in the story; the corresponding note below explains why the event was important.

Assign students the questions at the end of the chapter, telling them to choose what they believe are the three most useful questions. The follow-up discussion is about not only why they chose those questions, but also what makes them good questions. Also, allow students time to discuss their responses to the questions.

Require students to develop questions about a text or passage they will read but which you know they will find difficult. Have them read through it, then ask them to generate questions about specific passages or even words that would help them better understand the meaning of the text or the author's purpose. It helps to demonstrate this for the students, as this gives them permission to admit they do not understand something.

Offer students a variety of what I call "question sets" to help them generate more sophisticated questions about, for example, cause and effect. On the board, write something like, "What is the effect of *a* on *b* when *c* is removed?" Another, less algebraic set that I often use is, **"Who** does **what** to **whom, why, how do they do that**—and **so what** (i.e., why is that important)?" Replacing these letters or words with characters, events, or groups provides students with the structure they must internalize as they learn to ask these questions themselves. In a social studies class, for example, students might translate one of the above questions into: What did the Nazis do to the Jews? Why did they do it? How did they go about it? And what do their actions tell us about the German culture at that time and human nature in general?

Teach students to ask a range of questions for different purposes.

Not all questions are created equal. Though there are some, such as the "reporter's questions" (Who? What? When? Where? Why? How?), that can be adapted to any situation, some are more effective in specific situations or when used to understand particular types of texts. The questions the American history teacher asks when students read Jonathan Edwards' "Sinners in the Hands of an Angry God" would necessarily differ from those the American literature teacher down the hall would ask if his students were reading the same text, as they would if the science teacher and social studies teachers were both having students read about the subject of Darwin and evolution in their respective classes. Thus it is important for students in each subject area to learn the questions and strategies for asking and using those questions in the respective disciplines. Questions about the behavior of particles or the brain in the science or health classes would not necessarily be phrased or used the same way as questions about the behavior of characters in a story or historical event, yet all such questions are essential skills in those disciplines. The following suggestions offer guidance in teaching students to ask different kinds of questions:

> **Comprehension:** Students are merely trying to understand the basics in this case, much like the reporter who wants "just the facts, ma'am." In this instance, students are asking the "Reporter's Questions," also known as the "Five Ws and an H": who, what, when, where, why, and how. Some questions, such as those that begin with *why*, are more analytical, though they can obviously play a key role in comprehension.

> **Analysis:** When analyzing, one seeks to grasp the functions of and relationship between the parts that make up the whole of an experiment, poem, article, or infographic, which combines words and data in a visual form such as a graph. Such questions would focus on the *how* and the *why*, or the nature of the relationship between various characters or elements. In history, one asks, "How did the influx of people during the Gold Rush change the culture of the West?" In the science class, students learn to ask questions that will help them determine how one variable (e.g., force) affects another (e.g., mass). The language arts teacher asks such questions as, "How did the character feel about the war after he discovered the sniper he shot was his own brother?"

Evaluation: These questions assess the value or quality of information, a character, an object, or a process. Often, though not always, one has generated or gathered a collection of something—data, interpretations, even questions—that needs to be sorted out, by choosing the most viable or valuable. In such cases, the student must learn to ask such questions as, "Which of the following is the most viable interpretation based on the data I have gathered?" In science classes, students would ask a different question, one meant to evaluate the quality of data, such as "Which data is most important (or reliable)?"

Definition: It often seems that students, even those in Advanced Placement classes, charge ahead with little concern for the actual definitions of terms and concepts, ignoring what they don't understand and building their interpretation on what they do. Questions of definition are not limited to the meanings of individual words but also include phrases and concepts which may be unfamiliar or used in a novel way. Students need to learn to pause and ask such questions as, "How is the author using that particular word (or phrase)?" "What does the author mean when he describes a character as 'flat'?" or "What other possible meanings of the word *democratic* does this text include when it refers to 'democratic reforms'?"

Classification: Most academic subjects require students to classify information, data, and other content. Whether it is types of conflicts in an English class, different diseases in a health class, or a range of theories in an economics class, students need strategies for sorting; questions offer a useful approach. Questions include, "What are the qualities or features common among these different people?" "How are the different elements similar and different?" "What are the key features that distinguish these different people, groups, results, or objects?"

Ask students questions throughout the reading process.

The reading process is broken down into three phases: before, during, and after. Many in the English Language Learner community favor what might be considered an alternative approach—into, through, and beyond—though these are not specific to reading or asking questions. Still, it is a sequence I find useful in a different way than before-during-after (BDA). The main point is that there are these points along the way, moments in the process of learning when students' needs differ based on their own skills and the nature of the texts they are trying to read. BDA offers a structure the teacher can use (and get students to internalize) with any text, and its flexibility prevents it from losing its value since the questions you or students are asking at each stop along the way inevitably differ according to the needs of the assignment and the nature of the text. Here are some sample questions students find useful throughout the process:

Before: These questions tend to focus on accessing background knowledge ("What do you know about sleep?" the health teacher asks, while down the hall the English teacher poses the question, "What do you know about the United States in the 1960s in the South?). Other questions at this time center on the demands and conventions specific to text types ("What questions does it help to ask when reading a poem?" "What features do you pay most attention to when reading a map?" "What strategies should you use when reading a primary source document?"). Other questions might seek to draw the student into the text, emphasizing a more personal connection through the students' own experiences ("What was your neighborhood like when you were a little kid? Did you have curious characters on your street?" "Did anyone see *The Lord of the Rings*? If you did, who are the main characters and what role do they play in the story?")

During: Questions during this phase of the reading process tend to focus on several areas: monitoring comprehension, achieving your reading goal(s), and troubleshooting your own understanding when it breaks down. This is a more flexible, nuanced part of the process that is different for each reader, as some will understand what others do not. Questions during this process focus on determining which details are relevant to your purpose question. Thus, if students are reading to understand the causes of the 1929 stock market crash, they will use questions to evaluate the importance of information relative to that goal. A student might ask, "How might x have led to the sell-off?" In a health class, the student reading about adolescent sleep needs might pause to ask, "I know that the chapter said earlier on that teens need nine hours of sleep a night, but how does that contribute to growth as it says here?" Other questions that emerge while reading are useful in what are sometimes called "fix-up" situations akin to breaking down on the side of the road: You are reading along, understanding everything, then suddenly you can't move forward. In such situations, students need to learn to pull over onto the side of the road and start asking questions like, "Where did my comprehension break down?" "What caused me to not understand the text at that point?" "What do I need to know—the meaning of a word? the value of a symbol? the meaning of a phrase that the author is repeatedly using?—to get back up and running so I can understand and finish reading this text?"

After: The first thing to ask is whether you can answer your initial purpose question. If you were reading to understand what allowed people to survive extreme situations, can you answer that question when you finish? If you can, you can move on to more sophisticated questions and concerns; if you cannot, you might ask, "What part of the question do I still not understand and which part(s) of the text should I reread so I can answer my purpose question?" More advanced readers at this point might ask follow-up questions about the author's rhetorical or literary style, seeking to understand how the author structured his argument or how these elements contribute to the meaning of the work as a whole.

Teach specific question strategies.

Effective readers are strategic readers, evaluating each textual encounter like a skilled mechanic trying to diagnose and solve the problems of a particular car. At their disposal are a wide range of tools and techniques they have learned, but mostly they draw on certain questions they have learned to make sense of the sounds and troubles they encounter in the process of "reading" the car. Research on reading has yielded several questioning strategies that prove effective in a range of situations. Students need to learn not only *how* to use each one through direct and guided instruction, but also *when* to use each one. Here I summarize several of the most common questioning strategies:

QAR (Question–Answer Relationships)

QAR emphasizes the relationship between readers, the text, and their prior knowledge. This strategy works well with kids but requires some time to fully sink in as kids need to learn to distinguish between and identify different types of information

Baran creates a QAR poster for us to post
and refer to in a reading strategies class.

in the text. What *are* the QARs? They are four different types
of questions used to find answers in the text (Rafael 1986):

> **Right There Questions:** The answer to these questions
> can be found in the text, "right there" on the page.
> An example from a novel would be, "What crime was
> Tom Robinson accused of in *To Kill a Mockingbird?*" The
> question can be answered using words from the text itself.

> **Think and Search Questions:** These questions require the
> reader to make an inference based on different elements
> of the text. The reader considers these different
> elements and how they go together, and answers in her
> own words. An example of such a question would be,
> "What kind of a man was Atticus Finch?"

> **Author and You Questions:** Readers cannot find the
> answer to such questions in the text but must combine
> what they know with what the author says. An example
> of this type of question would be, "Why does Scout
> have a difficult time with her transition to school?" The
> answer draws on both what the author says and our own
> knowledge of human nature.

On Your Own Questions: Students generate their own questions in response to what they read. Such questions arise naturally, the answer coming not from the book but from the reader's own mind or sources other than the book that inspired the question. A student reading *To Kill a Mockingbird*, for example, might wonder, "What causes someone to take a stand in opposition to everyone else in their community?"

Vacca and Vacca (2005) suggest the following sequence for teaching QARs in the content areas:

1. Introduce the concept of QARs.

2. Assign students several short passages from the textbook.

3. Continue the second day by practicing with short passages.

4. Review briefly on the third day.

5. Apply the QAR strategy to actual content area assignments.

Reciprocal Teaching

Reciprocal Teaching (Palinscar & Brown 1984) combines questioning with other comprehension strategies and culminates in a discussion about the text at hand. While the teacher plays a more prominent role early on, helping students to master the techniques, the goal is a student who has internalized these strategies and can use them independently. The four strategic activities are Generate Questions, Summarize, Predict, and Clarify, each of which requires the use of various questions. A sample sequence for a text, which could be either literary or informational, would be:

- Choose the portion of the text that is appropriate for these activities, one that requires such robust support.

- Develop questions about the text.

- Make predictions about what the author will say, what the characters will do, and how the story will unfold or end.

- Clarify the meaning of key words, ideas, and sentences students may not immediately understand.

Keep in Mind! Students from other cultures, as well as those who lack confidence, perhaps owing to some learning challenge, can find it difficult to ask questions. Indeed, some students have been raised not to question authority or adults.

ReQUEST

ReQUEST is a versatile strategy that helps students at all levels, including ELLs, as it allows students to develop their own questions in response to what they read. Students become active readers who, through their own questions, engage with the text in an attempt to comprehend it. The procedure is as follows:

- In small groups or pairs, both students and teachers read a particular portion of the text. For difficult texts or students who are struggling, this might mean selecting only one sentence at a time.

- Generate questions about the passage for the teacher to answer. These should be academic questions, the sort of questions that might appear on a test or that would arise in a class discussion led by the teacher.

- The teacher then poses questions about that same excerpt.

- Students and teacher alternate, repeating these two previous steps for as long as it is appropriate and effective.

Adam and Travis generate questions about and annotate a poem prior to discussing it in class.

- The teacher asks students to make predictions about the outcome or meaning of the text, allowing students to speculate about these questions and explain the basis of their prediction.

- Students read the rest of the assigned text, keeping in mind their predictions and other background knowledge they have learned.

- Students participate in a class discussion led by the teacher, who uses additional follow-up questions about the text to help students understand and elaborate on what they read.

QtA (Question the Author)

QtA teaches students to be active, attentive readers by showing them how effective readers ask questions throughout the reading process. QtA strives to model the questions students must ask if they are to move beyond basic comprehension and into a deeper understanding of the text at hand. In Salinger's *The Catcher in the Rye*, the narrator Holden Caulfield says that he wished he could call up an author and ask him what he was thinking when he wrote a certain passage—not unlike QtA. This strategy requires students to formulate challenging, substantial questions they might ask the author in an attempt to grasp not only the meaning of the text but also the author's intent and the important ideas in the text. The process has several main steps (Beck, et al. 1997, p. 8):

- The teacher intervenes at selected points in the text.

- The teacher then poses queries to prompt students to consider information in the text.

- Students respond by contributing ideas, which may be built upon, refined, or challenged by other students and by the teacher.

- Students and the teacher work collaboratively, interacting to grapple with ideas and build understanding.

QtA requires deliberate planning on the teacher's part. If done properly, this strategy demands that the teacher read the text ahead of time, determining which portions the class should stop and create queries for prior to discussing them. The questions come into play before and during reading. Vacca and Vacca (2005, p. 135) offer several sample questions.

Before reading, ask such initial questions as these:

- What is the author trying to say?

- What is the author's message?

- What is the author talking about?

During the reading, students and teachers can ask such follow-up questions as these:

- This is what the author says, but what does it mean?

- How does this text segment connect with what the author has already said?

- Does the author make sense here?

- Did the author explain this clearly?

- What's missing? What do we need to find out?

After they finish reading, students use their queries and the subsequent responses to discuss the text. Beck and McKeown (2006) emphasize the importance of "discussion moves," which they describe as "actions that teachers take to help orchestrate students' participation and the development of ideas" (p. 92). Here is a list of their "moves," followed by a brief description:

Marking: Teachers indicate explicitly or through strategic emphasis (tone of voice, particular phrases, paraphrase) that some idea in the text is important. For example, a teacher says, in response to Ellen's remark about a text, "Let's pause for a second and look at what Ellen just said about this idea in the text, because that was an important observation."

Turning back: This action comes in two forms: turning back to text and turning back to students. Turning back to text redirects students back into the text to solve comprehension problems. Instead of dismissing a student's response as wrong, this move allows the teacher to ask, "Is that what the author said?" Or, the teacher might pose more pointed questions that redirect the students back into the text, asking, for example, "Does the author say what caused x to happen?" or "Does the author explain why she thinks x is important?" The other move, turning back to students, asks students to elaborate on and clarify their responses to the text. When, for example, a student does not fully respond to a previous question or explain his answer, the teacher would ask, "What does it mean when the king refers to the citizens as his 'children'?" More sophisticated moves include asking students to make connections between the text they are discussing and others they have read: "How is the Vietnam War in this story similar to or different from the Iraq War you studied in World History recently?" In my classes, we are typically exploring a larger question or subject (e.g., "What does it take to be a survivor?") which I will regularly use as a way of turning back to students the discussion about the text we are reading. The primary idea is to make the students responsible for wrestling with the text and prevent teachers from taking over the thinking.

Revoicing: During discussions, students may struggle to find the words to explain what they mean, particularly those students with language difficulties or who lack the academic language needed to articulate their ideas. "Rephrasing" or "revoicing" is a way to help: "So what you are saying, Maria, is that the author used 'image words'—about the color of the sky and his clothing—to suggest that the boy in the story is slowly turning to stone in response to his brother's death." In this way we shape the student's language, clarify her ideas, sharpen her thinking, and give the rest of the class discussion ideas for further exploration.

Recapping: Recapping is a way of reiterating and clarifying what students know before they move ahead to other aspects or portions of the assigned text. Teachers do this as part of the discussion, saying "So what we know at this point is that x leads to y because of of z, which is important because . . ." Students, too, can do the recapping, learning or reinforcing in the process those summarizing skills they have focused on at other points in the course.

Modeling: Teachers use these discussion moves to show students how they arrive at their understanding of difficult texts. Such modeling should not be superficial but authentic, offering guidance in how effective readers (in this case, the teacher) solve the problems they encounter while reading. In my English class, for example, as we discussed the short story "The Sniper," about an IRA sniper, I would model for students how I arrived at my understanding of his emotional conflict: "Early on, it says something about him having the 'eyes of a fanatic,' and living like an ascetic. These are words that are all about faith and devotion, the kinds of words that you would use to describe a priest. As I am reading these words, and come to the part where he feels remorse after killing the other sniper, I ask why he is having a crisis of conscience. This makes me realize that what he did is in conflict with what he believes." On other occasions, if I know a student has arrived at a profound insight, I will often ask her to model for the class how she arrived at that interpretation, what questions she asked, and what strategies she used.

Annotating: Verbal annotations add to those portions of the text that seem incomplete or unclear due to lack of details. The teacher—or, in some cases, a student—fills in the gaps in the text where the author may, for example, assume the reader knows what happened or why something is important. In my senior English class, students reading *Oedipus* tend to forget that Christianity and Jesus arrived roughly five hundred years after the play was written, so Sophocles' plays, performed in amphitheaters, were the equivalent of today's megachurches, where customs and values were clarified and conveyed. Thus as we read portions of the story, I will verbally annotate the text to identify the details related to faith. And then, rather than let such remarks stand as lectures, I ask students to connect what I have said to themselves, to other works we have read, or to the world in which they live.

KWL

KWL (Ogle 1992) works well across content areas and different types of texts, giving teachers and students a flexible strategy that benefits all students. KWL stands for:

- What do I already **K**now about this subject?
- What do I **W**ant to learn about this subject?
- What did I **L**earn—or still need to learn—about this subject?

What I Already **K**now	What I **W**ant to Learn	What I **L**earned

Typically used in conjunction with some sort of organizer with a column for each question, KWL offers guidance in accessing prior knowledge (what you already know about the subject) and getting students to think about the subject ahead (what you want to know). It moves the brain to "prime the pump" for learning by activating certain parts and functions in the brain that are related to comprehension and retention.

The strategy can backfire, however, if the teacher doesn't prepare carefully; if students do not care about or already know something about the subject, they may resist the activity, making the whole experience one of frustration and futility. To avoid such a result, prepare students and evaluate whether this is the right question strategy to use on this particular text. I often talk openly and specifically about the importance and role of prior knowledge in understanding what we read, taking time when appropriate to enhance or add to my students' background knowledge about a subject through supplemental readings, discussion, or passages of video carefully chosen to inform. Here are some suggestions about how to use this strategy effectively:

- Give everyone a copy of the organizer (see page 76) and ask them to complete the first two columns (*What I Already Know* and *What I Want to Learn*) on their own. After this step, they can get into groups for an initial prereading discussion, during which they might think of new elements to add to their column. As an alternative, you could facilitate a whole-class discussion, having students use their organizers to help them participate.

- Give everyone a copy of the organizer but put a transparency of the same organizer on your overhead (or project on your SMART Board) and use it to facilitate a whole-class discussion, telling students to add these details to their own as you fill it in.

- Ask students to generate (or work with them to generate) categories into which the author of the assigned text is likely to organize information. Such predictions prepare students not only to read but also to think about the subject and activate those parts of the brain that organize and make sense of information as it comes in.

- Return to the organizer throughout the reading process, using it to check on what your students still need to learn. Have students write to reflect on their emerging understanding of the subject based on what they thought earlier and what they have read so far. You might put up sentence frames such as, "Initially I thought x, but now I realize y. What made me realize this was..."

- Generate new—enduring, remaining, emerging— questions when students finish reading the assigned text. Students might be asked to make speculative responses to these questions based on what they have learned so far, then reread the text with these new questions in mind.

- Use the completed notes as the basis for various follow-up activities such as a discussion or short writing assignment in which students synthesize what they learned about the subject and their questions and what they regard as most important.

5. Visualize Texts

All great readers are makers of movies. They take in the key details and transform them, often without realizing it, into sounds and images, colors and shapes, all of which combine in the theater of the reader's imagination to reveal connections, characters, and processes that were difficult to discern on the one-dimensional space of the page. This process of visualizing, while applicable to students at all grade levels and in all subject areas, makes great demands on the reader. Don't let the idea of visualization fool you into thinking this a strategy only for elementary school or struggling readers, for it is only when the material resists easy understanding that teachers should ask students to "draw the action," "show the process," or "illustrate the connections." I'm as likely to use this strategy in my AP Literature class with seniors as I am with my college prep freshmen. Besides, it transforms the energy of the class: There's nothing like a group of seniors creating abstract art about *Crime and Punishment* to represent the key ideas in the story to get a better understanding of them.

Visualization supports both struggling and advanced readers in several ways. First, it allows students to see connections

Guiding Principles

- Make abstract or unfamiliar topics comprehensible.
- Summarize, analyze, and organize events, processes, and stories.
- Reveal and communicate connections and big ideas in texts.
- Synthesize and extend students' thinking about texts.

among characters, ideas, or events that are not obvious at first glance. By asking students to represent those connections, teachers force kids to go inside the text and, after evaluating which details are most important and analyzing how they relate to each other, communicate those connections using patterns, symbols, diagrams, or other graphic techniques. Visualization also gives students—and teachers—a different way to summarize and make inferences about texts. By transforming what is on the page into something on a screen or sheet of paper, students process the material at deeper levels, thus improving both comprehension and retention. This process of visually representing content synthesizes many different aspects of reading, creating a powerful schema that helps integrate new information into the memory, and giving the students a way to remember and retrieve the information in the present and future. Finally, visualization enables students to take what is unfamiliar or invisible to them and see and better understand what is going on, where it is set, and what it all means.

Jessica uses details from Maya Angelou's poem "I Know Why the Caged Bird Sings" to represent the poem's meaning.

Make abstract or unfamiliar topics comprehensible.

When we struggle to understand something, then have that breakthrough moment, we typically exclaim, "Oh, I see!" Initially, we lacked a sense of what a person was talking about, having no sense of what it looked like—what it *was*. This is the same experience we often have when reading a text that is about unfamiliar subjects or abstract ideas. We simply don't know what it looks like. Obviously this involves some background knowledge. Here, though, the question is how to help students understand such material by visualizing it. It would be silly to offer only words about how to help students *see* things, so instead I will focus more on representative examples from my class and explain how these might apply to your own class.

Visualization comes in a variety of forms, including imagining, drawing, acting out, diagramming, and representing through other visual means such as timelines, graphs, and maps. When my students are reading something that, because it is abstract or unfamiliar to them, calls for visualization, I try these sources:

YouTube and relevant videos provide background knowledge to help students see and hear what they are reading about. For example, when reading a short story about an Irish republican sniper, it became clear that my students had no point of reference for Ireland, the IRA, and so forth. A quick search on YouTube turned up an excellent seven-minute video that told the story of the "Troubles" through the murals painted all over Northern Ireland, interspersed with news reports about the events depicted. The National Holocaust Memorial Museum site offers online interviews and documentaries that provide students with a visual sense of time and place prior to reading a book like *Anne Frank: The Diary of a Young Girl* or Elie Wiesel's *Night*. Shakespeare is difficult for students; to prepare them for *Romeo and Juliet*, I searched YouTube and found an anime (Japanese animation) version that was five minutes long. I played the entire video (without sound, as it was in Japanese) and asked them write a summary of the story after watching it. Here is a glimpse:

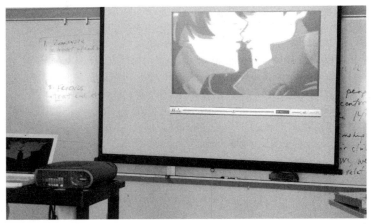

YouTube offers useful clips to help students visualize what they read. Here we watched a short anime film based on *Romeo and Juliet*.

Google Images offers excellent help for providing examples of what unfamiliar words or events look like. When reading a novel, we start a PowerPoint document and add images from Google Images that help us see what we could not previously understand. When a setting or word we don't know comes up, I fire up the LCD projector and go on Google Images to search with the class for a *curandera* to see what comes up. The screen fills with ten different images of traditional women from Central and South America curing people with herbs. I copy and paste the selected image onto the PowerPoint slide and type "Curandera" across the top. We revisit the images as we work our way through the book or at the end as a review. Here is a sample slide of a railroad bridge, something my suburban kids could not imagine:

Google Image Search helps us visualize characters, places, and events.

Metaphors, analogies, and similes ask people to use what they do know to understand what they don't. When studying a subject like the French Revolution or Industrial Revolution, students often find it hard to read about these subjects because they have no frame of reference. The history teacher can help students read about and understand the French Revolution by asking them to complete analogies such as this: *The French Revolution was to France as* _____ *was to the United States.* Depending on the time available and students' needs, the teacher can ask students to depict this analogy using images. In my own class, prior to reading a short story set during the Vietnam War, I gave students the following assignment:

Sample assignment

Authors often use figurative speech, especially metaphors, to convey more complicated ideas. "War is hell" is a perfect example of such a metaphor. This assignment asks you to think about that statement, what it means, and how it relates to the story we are reading. The quotation comes from both Napoleon (1860) and General William Tecumseh Sherman, a Union general during the American Civil War, who said, "There is many a boy here to-day who looks on war as all glory, but, boys, it is hell" (1880). Over 600,000 Americans lost their lives during the Civil War, more than all those killed in all the other American wars combined.

Do each of the following steps to complete this assignment:

1. Generate associations with the saying, "War is hell." Brainstorm ideas and connections— whatever comes to mind!—related to each individual word. If you get stuck, you might try looking at a thesaurus.

2. Watch excerpt from *Dear America: Letters from Vietnam*. As you watch, add details, images, and words to your brainstorm in Step 1.

3. Share your ideas, taking at least five ideas from others in your group and adding them to your own notes.

4. Organize your ideas into clusters around the words or use some other visually interesting format. Consider adding images, colors, quotations, clip art, magazine cutouts, or original artwork.

5. Add details from the short story, "Where Have You Gone, Charming Billy?"

Jesus generates ideas as he tries to represent the concept that "war is hell."

Draw the setting or action to help students see what it looks like. When reading an older book like Homer's *Odyssey*, one set in a place that students cannot imagine, they can use details from the text to illustrate what the place looks like. Such concrete representations help students see and understand what they are reading by taking them *into* the text to find the actual words they can translate into a real image. When my students read "The Most Dangerous Game" by Richard Connell, a short story set on an island, they draw the setting to understand not only what it looks like but also how it relates to the plot.

James and Samantha present their map of the story "The Most Dangerous Game" based on a close reading of the text.

About this assignment, one of my students wrote, "Our project helped us connect and respond to the literature. We had to list the main events and ideas of the story and describe why they were important. That helps us use descriptive language and imagery. This project really helped us review our reading and use descriptive language, and our own impressions and understandings to interpret it."

Summarize, analyze, and organize events, processes, and stories.

Once students have made their initial efforts to understand what they are reading, they can move ahead into and through the text. After they finish reading the assigned passage or text, they need a way to put the pieces together. Whether they need to summarize or analyze the separate elements of an historical event, a process, or a story, students can gain considerable insight into their reading through visualizing. Here are several different ways to approach using visualization to summarize and analyze what happens.

Transform the plot into a comic strip or skit. In his sophomore English class, Tim Larkin has students break down a scene from *Macbeth* first as a tableau (a freeze-frame of the key moment in the scene), then take a photo strip panel which they turn into a comic with captions.

A more economical and efficient alternative is to have students identify the main events in a story, and then, after explaining *why* those are the main events, arrange those events into a comic strip with drawings based on details from the story and captions that derive from the text. This graphic approach to the material provides substantial support for English Language Learners as well as those who need to process what they read through different senses. Instead of turning them loose, I use my LCD projector to show samples of comic books I found online; this allows us to talk about the conventions of the comic-book format.

Students in Tim Larkin's sophomore class transform their acting into a comic strip to help them understand *Macbeth*.

Students in my freshman English class adapt "The Sniper" into a comic strip to help them identify and examine the key events in the story.

Graphic organizers can provide useful ways to visually summarize and examine events across time. As an alternative, you can use the whiteboard and sticky notes as the example below illustrates. The idea here is to choose a graphic organizer that will help students see how the story unfolds, and how the character evolves. In the sample below, you see a figure representing a bridge, the central metaphor in *Bless Me, Ultima*. On one side is Antonio's family and all that goes with his more traditional life; on the other side, school and a more modern future. We return and keep adding to this diagram as we continue to read the story.

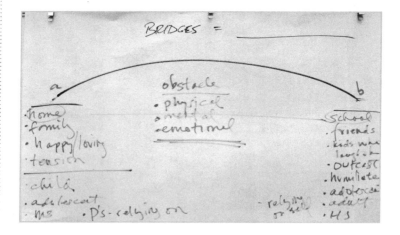

A variation, as mentioned, is to create an organizer such as a time line on the board so students see how events correspond to each other and themes develop across time. In this case, I divided the organizer into two levels ("What happened?" on top, "Why is it important?" on the bottom) to get students to think about the importance of the event. Students had two sticky notes, one blue (for the top), the other yellow (for the bottom); after filling each one in, they went to the board to figure out where it should go in relation to the others. The completed time line allowed us to see the big picture and then discuss how the story unfolded. We kept it up for the rest of the week to use as a visual record of the story and our thinking.

Visual models allow students to break up a story or analyze an idea into a more visual form. Sometimes these models might be pyramids to represent a hierarchy; other times students choose more organic visual forms. In the example that follows, students needed help seeing not only how the characters related to each other, but also how they connected to the ideas in the novel *Bless*

Me, Ultima. I told students they could come up with any way they wanted to create a visual representation of the stages of life and the characters that were associated with each stage. This group chose to use a pyramid.

Reveal and communicate connections and big ideas in texts.

What distinguishes remarkable minds from the rest are the connections they make between seemingly unrelated ideas. In science, literature, mathematics, or the social sciences, the great minds notice what escapes the rest of us. Often, when they discuss how they make these connections, they speak of "seeing" connections, of visualizing the problem so they can consider it from multiple sides. If we are to teach our students to see these connections, patterns, or big ideas played out in the texts they read, we must show them how it is done and provide them the opportunity to practice and master it. Here are a few techniques that you can use to help students see these deeper connections within and among the texts they read in your class:

Highlight the text, using particular colors to code the author's use of certain words or grammatical structures. Winston Churchill, who was dyslexic, had a teacher who color-coded various structures and features of written texts so young Winston could *see* how language behaved and thereby better understand what he read as well as master the finer points of rhetoric. This is far from a remedial strategy: I frequently have students in my AP Literature class use highlighters to reveal for themselves a poet's use of imagery or other literary devices. Once they see how the yellow highlights fall in a recurring pattern in specific places, they can then study those to see not only what it means, but also how the poet achieved that meaning. As a variation, I use the highlighting or color-coding features in PowerPoint or Word to draw students' attention to certain aspects of the text I display on the screen using my LCD projector.

Graphic organizers reveal connections, giving students the support they need to see and elaborate on them. In *Romeo and Juliet*, for example, connections abound but can be difficult to see if students are struggling to understand the text. When I want students to see the different choices available to characters in *Romeo and Juliet*, to analyze these conflicting options and the reasons why characters choose the ones they do, I turn to a visual tool such as the Decision Tree (Burke 2002). It allows students to see that Shakespeare as the author has options, as do his characters. It also allows them to see how each of those would play out in a more visual way.

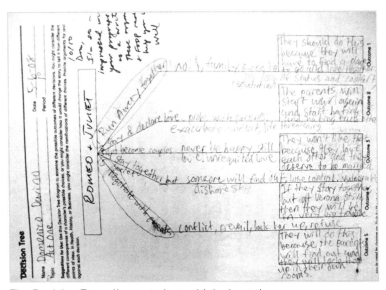

The Decision Tree allows students think about the decisions both the author and characters have.

On other occasions, I want students to consider a subject or character from different perspectives and, in doing so, see how much more complex the character or situation is. For example, if I am teaching a collection of poems that explore a certain subject, I will use an organizer such as Target Notes (Burke 2002) to help students consolidate their observations about the subject through the poems.

Illustrations and visual representations come in many forms: graphs, charts, diagrams, and, of course, drawings. As my freshmen finished reading *The Odyssey*, they needed a way to identify and convey their understanding of the big ideas in the story. Time was short, but we needed a good way to work with this demanding text that would help them better grasp what they had read. Suddenly I thought of the ancient Bayeux tapestry, which is a long embroidered cloth depicting both the events that led up to the 1066 Norman invasion of England and the invasion itself. What struck me about it was the design: it is broken up into episodes (some call it the first graphic novel), with the action summarized in

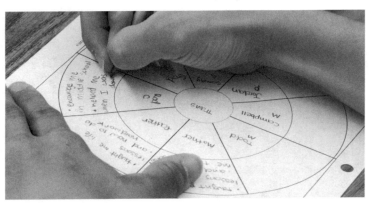

Students reading *Bless Me, Ultima* used graphic organizers to identify and generate details about Antonio's different "teachers," then used the same organizer to connect the novel to their own lives.

the main (middle) space, and framed along the top and bottom with images and words that offer commentary (i.e., annotations) on the events depicted in the middle. This seemed a perfect activity to help students see how *The Odyssey* was organized; moreover, it allowed them to offer, through the annotations in the top and bottom spaces, comments on the action in their assigned book of *The Odyssey*. Students then presented and explained their visual narrative and commentary:

Yaz and Ilan present their portion of our *Odyssey* tapestry to the class, explaining how the details of their drawing correspond with the story.

Just about every subject involves reading graphs, charts, maps, and diagrams, many of which are made up of colors, symbols, and other features. In addition to teaching students how to *read* such visual explanations, teachers might consider having students *create* them. The health teacher might have students visually depict the information about sleep and school performance on a graph. The economics teacher can ask students to transform the assigned reading into a pie chart or other diagram that illustrates how the market changes over time. The photo on the next page shows some of the different ways students can visually represent the plot of a story.

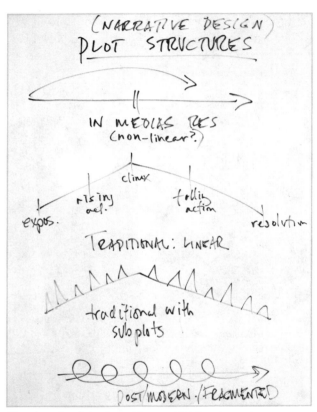

Sketches from the board in my AP Literature class where we examined different narrative patterns, then applied these to the stories we read.

Synthesize and extend students' thinking about texts.

When students finish reading, the work with that text is not over. Visualization offers powerful avenues for thinking about and expressing one's understanding of the assigned text. Sometimes these assignments help to extend thinking about a text; on other occasions, the purpose of such assignments is to direct the student back *into* the text to improve comprehension and synthesize ideas through more holistic, visual means. Here are a few samples of how I do this in my own class:

Art projects, often best offered as an option since not everyone is inclined to do the necessary work, provide exciting opportunities that tap into students' other intelligences and strengths. Projects might include collages, paintings, photo essays, or mixed media works; whatever the form, the product should be quality work through which the student expresses both understanding and insight. Here is an example of a painting done by a student who read Cormac McCarthy's *The Road*, an apocalyptic novel, as well as two other novels as part of a larger investigation into different views of the future.

Hanayo used her talents as a painter to synthesize the key ideas in three novels she read as part of her study of apocalyptic literature.

Photo essays are a new option to consider. I introduced the idea in the following assignment for my freshman class: "An essay is a person's attempt, usually through words, to tell a story, persuade another person, or explain something (an idea, a text, or an experience). This assignment asks you to use images (and PowerPoint) to explain your final thoughts about this unit's Big Question, 'What does it take to be a survivor?' It also requires you to learn how to use the computer in some new ways to communicate. For examples of photo essays, visit: http://www.time.com/time/photoessays." This assignment requires students to find images through Google Images and copy these into PowerPoint, then add commentary on the slide to explain how this image relates to the main idea of the student's photo essay. A new and exciting alternative source for such multimedia publications is http://www.realelibrary.com.

Students work in the lab to create their photo essays in which they examined the subject of survival through images and words.

Movies, while much more ambitious and complex, represent an increasingly new and viable alternative for students who think "in pictures" about the books they read. Creating such a movie typically requires additional thinking through visualization, namely brainstorming through storyboards where students sketch out the scenes and arrange their ideas. Because it is so demanding, this option is probably best as one of several choices; otherwise, you would have to spend much more time than you have available teaching students how to use the software to create and edit the film.

Francesca, Dylan, Jennifer, and Tessa create their presentation about their imaginary video game based on the short story "The Most Dangerous Game," which they then presented to the class.

6. Use a Range of Instructional Strategies to Enhance and Extend Comprehension

As humans we need variety—and not just because it's the spice of life. True, we grow easily bored when faced with seemingly endless repetition, feeling the monotony a slow form of torture that serves no purpose. It's also true, however, that we have gone too far, dismissing repetition as ineffective, a charge that would be challenged by every great artist who drew the same hand over and over 'til he got it right or any professional athlete who spent hours perfecting his free throw or honing her backhand. Yet when it comes to teaching a class full of kids with as many different learning styles as there are students, the need for instructional variety—a variety that promotes understanding and improved performance by tapping into students' different cognitive strengths—is clear and compelling. In this way, variation improves the mental dexterity of all students.

I offer this brief overview as an informal guide to these different strategies, hoping you will find it useful as a checklist, a menu you can use to remind yourself of the different ways you can approach content area reading instruction and to assess the effectiveness of your own current instructional choices. Looking at the list below, you might realize that you have been overemphasizing writing as a means of understanding the assigned texts, in which case you might consider doing a think-aloud to help students better understand the subject and the text itself. Each of these strategies comes with the seal of approval from years of research in all classes, at all levels, with all students.

Write About Texts.

Reading and writing involve many of the same key processes of constructing meaning, one of which (writing) is dedicated to creating what the other (reading) interprets. Both are, at their core, active processes through which the student makes sense of a subject or, in this case, a text. The methods listed below all have their place; it is up to you to choose the right one for a given instructional context. Whether students do this writing on the computer, in a notebook, or on sticky notes, butcher paper, or the page of the text itself matters little; the point is that when students read with pencils in hand, they are transformed into active readers engaged in the hunt for meaning and should use those pencils to dig down to the meaning of those big ideas that may, at first, elude them. You can incorporate writing into your reading instruction by offering students options such as these:

- Take notes in a notebook, through a structured note-taking form, or on butcher paper.

- Respond to the text by writing about the author's intent, as well as your own thoughts about, experiences with, or connections to the subject of the text you are reading.

- Write to learn about both the subject and the type of text you are reading; this might mean using the text you are reading as a model for your own poem, lab report, or op-ed column about a social issue or presidential candidate.

- Annotate the text by making notes in the margin of the text itself, jotting down questions and comments on sticky notes and placing those on the page near the subject under discussion, or make transparencies of the text and use overhead pens to mark them up prior to presenting to the class your reading of the text.

- Write a traditional summary or a variation such as a summary-response, in which you first identify, then respond to the key ideas in the text; a précis, in which you summarize the main ideas and then discuss the rhetorical means the author uses to make her point; or a paraphrase, in which you rewrite the original text in your own words.

Talk About Texts.

Learning is inherently social. We learn by watching, by asking others how they did something, by talking about what we did to solve a problem, and in the process, passing along our knowledge to others. Students consistently find that structured, effective discussion improves comprehension, engagement, and retention more than just about any other instructional technique. This doesn't mean telling the class to "Just talk for a few minutes about the chapter and share your thoughts about it." That will yield only accidental learning. Instead, you need to give students a specific task with discernible outcomes that they must complete within a short period of time, thus creating a sense of urgency that results in disciplined work. Other options include assigning people roles to play during the discussion or giving them time to do a particular task on their own (e.g., solve a problem, write a response, observe a process) prior to having a whole-class discussion. Here are the most common and, if implemented well, most effective ways to use discussion to improve reading comprehension:

- Whole-class discussion of the text affords opportunities for students to make observations about not only what the text means but also why they think this. During such a discussion, the teacher has several important roles to play. First, he or she needs to monitor the degree of participation; to this end, the teacher should consider using a seating chart to keep track of who participates and facilitate the discussion to include as many students as possible. Second, the teacher must monitor the quality of the discussion, asking clarifying and follow-up questions to ensure that the discussion does not get stuck at the surface level but extends into deeper issues and connections to the larger subject of the course and other texts the class has read. Finally, the teacher should structure the discussion to ensure that everyone has a way to contribute; this might mean having everyone take a few minutes to write their thoughts about the text at hand. This prevents the teacher from calling on kids who get that deer-in-the-headlights look of bafflement, and gives students a chance to gather their thoughts before they share them with the class, perhaps reading them if that makes them more comfortable. Some whole-class discussions have more formal guidelines such as the Socratic seminar or other discussion protocols.

- Small groups may include such structured techniques as Literature Circles or reciprocal teaching. In these small groups, which may be set up for one period or the duration of a unit (e.g., the study of *Hamlet*), students will do best if they have identified roles and specific goals to achieve. I also find it helps if students know they need to report out to the class their conclusions, coming to the class discussion prepared to explain and defend their interpretation of the text.

- Pairs offer the most efficient means of a quick discussion. Some research has found that even *one minute* of discussion has measurable benefits for reading comprehension if it follows those guidelines outlined above. Paired conversations tend to be more informal, as in, "Turn to your neighbor and compare your two interpretations of the text, noting the places where you had different opinions about what the author was saying."

• The think-pair-square-share method combines all of the above in a sequence that can take part or all of a class period. Students begin by thinking about the text after first reading and writing about it on their own. Then they move into pairs, discussing the text as directed by the teacher for the allotted period of time. Then they get into groups of four (i.e., the square) to compare and extend their discussion of the text, perhaps taking on at this point some new task the teacher assigns to add more complexity to the assignment. Finally, the group shares with the entire class, during which time the teacher facilitates the class discussion.

• Online discussions (which might include blogs, threaded discussions, Twitter, or a wiki) combine elements of talking and writing, forming something of a written conversation, but play to students' strengths and interests. In my English class, for example, freshmen participate in an online blog during one period in which they post comments and respond to others' ideas about the question, "Am I my brother's keeper?" as it applies to the novel *Of Mice and Men*.

Read Aloud.

Reading aloud is often dismissed as an elementary school technique, yet often my students tell me that hearing me read the text—whether a poem or a demanding text with many rhetorical flourishes—allows them to understand it better. We know how the text should sound, where the emphasis should come down, which part of the sentence should be subordinated to make room for the big idea that comes through at the end. We discern the speaker's or author's tone in a way that is difficult for students to do. Try the following to help students better understand what you assign them to read:

- Read aloud the directions for a difficult assignment or writing topic so you can emphasize the key details.

- Give a dramatic reading of a literary text, making sure to emphasize the words in the way the author intended or in a way you believe will otherwise help them better understand the text.

- Ask students to read along with the text you are reading aloud so they hear and see the text at the same time. This multi-modal approach helps all students internalize the cues you have picked up as a reader over the years.

- Choose students to read aloud, particularly those "drama kids" who love to get into the act. You can help students prepare to read aloud by giving them a copy of the pages to mark up with accents that show them where to emphasize certain words, or you might annotate the page to remind them what kind of tone to use.

- Single out just a line or passage to read aloud by way of drawing students' attention to its syntax or grammar, its ideas, or its imagery. Sometimes it's enough just to read aloud a passage to note the beauty of its language or the power of its imagery. Speeches such as the Gettysburg Address or passages from *Hamlet*, for example, beg to be read aloud.

Think Aloud.

Thinking aloud about texts is like orally annotating what the text is doing and what the teacher is doing as a reader. It's a bit like plugging a cord into a reader's head and listening to what goes through his mind as he tries to make sense of the text. Think of it as similar to one of those PBS shows on which an artist or piano player tells you what he is doing as he does it and then asks you to try the same. Think-alouds focus on the process of making meaning, and on the decisions the reader makes as he makes them. To incorporate this strategy into your class, try these options:

- Place a transparency of a text on the overhead so you can visually illustrate the process you follow as you make sense of a Shakespearean sonnet. When I do this, I typically mark it up to help my students see what I am saying as I do the think-aloud.

- Read aloud from the text, pausing to talk about the questions I am asking at that particular time or the choices I face given my current understanding of the text. The important thing is to go public about the steps you follow to arrive at your own understanding and, by making that process visible, show students how it's done.

- Teach as you talk about specific text elements and structures. For example, as I am reading aloud from a passage of a text in my class, I will note aloud that it is organized using a compare-contrast structure and will point out the signal words and other elements used. Every text has features that beg to be taught as examples. In a more advanced class, I will do the same thing except with subtle uses of irony or imagery that merit attention since students might not notice them on their own.

- Talk students through a text collaboratively, reading a passage and doing a think-aloud; then ask them to do the same with the text passage, taking time to pause and ask them to explain (to you or a partner) what went on, what problems they encountered, and how they solved them. If someone stumbles on a problem, consider taking time to read it aloud and do a think-aloud for the class.

- Go public with your own process when your comprehension breaks down. In my AP literature class, for example, I came into class one day and said, "I don't know about you guys but that Emily Dickinson poem really stumped me last night. I read it about twenty times! I kept getting stuck on this one part where she says... Then I thought, maybe I'm not asking the right questions, so I tried this..., then that. Finally, I realized I was making an assumption about who the speaker in the poem was and that this assumption was very wrong. I assumed the speaker was not only a human but Dickinson herself when in fact it was..."

Use Graphic Organizers.

As we face students with a wider range of learning needs, we need a wider range of tools to use. Graphic organizers give students a way to get inside the texts they read and work with, to make connections between the ideas in that text. The important thing to remember is that the organizer is not the end result but the beginning, the tool that prepares students to write about or discuss the assigned text or the topic. I vary the way I incorporate them, depending on the instructional needs of students or the context of the task. In general, however, I follow this process:

- Give each student a handout with the graphic organizer on it, asking them to complete it on their own or with a few other students; sometimes this is a one-two step: they complete the organizer first on their own, then move into groups to add to or discuss it.

- Provide each group with a transparency of the tool, which they must complete and present to the class. This might mean giving them a Frayer diagram, for example—an organizer divided into four large blocks, with a small circle or ellipse in the center of the page that names the topic under study. (See Google images for a variety of models of the Frayer diagram.) Students then use each of the squares to organize their notes from four separate readings, each of which represents a different perspective on the assigned topic.

• Allow students to work on butcher paper in much the same way they did with the transparency. Butcher paper offers kids a bigger space to work on and an opportunity to be more collaborative while working. They draw the organizer on the paper themselves or come up with their own organizer to represent their ideas (e.g., a cycle to represent the different stages of a journey a character goes through or the stages of a cell).

• Project an organizer up onto the screen or whiteboard and use this to facilitate the class discussion of a text, asking students to copy it down as you build it. This gives structure to the class discussion of the text, complementing other strategies such as modeling and thinking aloud. It can also serve as a means of synthesizing everyone's ideas in the final segment of the class if all the students use the same organizer and now share what they came up with. You can add their ideas to the organizer, asking questions to clarify and extend their thinking, then make them a copy or keep it on hand to refer to in subsequent discussions.

Create Visual Representation.

It helps students to *see* what most texts say, to bring to their reading a visual element that was so present when they read picture books as children. These strategies are some of the most powerful in our arsenal; in fact, a quick glance at the instructional strategies in this chapter reveals that most of them have some visual component. When thinking about how to use visual representation to improve reading, consider these options:

- Ask students to "draw the action" to help them see what is happening in the chapter, sequence, or story. This can mean having them draw a comic or the setting in a story to better see what it looks like, relying on the details from the text itself.

- Provide or project art or other visual images (from the textbook, online resources, or other sources) that complement the written text and help students see what they are reading about. These might include photographs or art from the Depression while reading about it in a social studies class, or looking at graphs and charts that visually depict what the science textbook is saying about an abstract subject like gravity.

- Show targeted excerpts from videos that illustrate what students are reading or prepare them, prior to reading the actual text, by helping them see what a certain process, person, or event looked like.

- Request that students come up with their own visual explanation of material, creating a visual metaphor, graph, or chart to summarize and synthesize the different ideas and perspectives in one or more texts.

- Project a map to provide visual structure, for example, to a historical movement in time across space. The teacher, in conjunction with the class, would add to this map (or series of maps that reflect the stages in, for example, westward migration) as they read and gather more details.

Develop Anticipation Guides.

These guides prepare students to read by giving them something to look for, a rudder to guide them through the text. Some of these guides are more oriented toward preparing the students to read, getting their brains primed to think about a subject by asking questions about the subject. In short, they pose questions through one form or another in order to improve comprehension and increase retention of material. I have had success with all the following:

- Create a questionnaire about a subject students may or may not know about prior to reading. These questionnaires might focus on assumptions and prejudices; they flush out obsolete or inaccurate knowledge and make room for the new, revised information. Such questionnaires, sometimes referred to as "opinionaires," can be quickly created about issues related to health, historical events or figures, subjects central to novels, or more controversial subjects such as evolution. Students can respond to them themselves, use them to interview others—or do both.

- Develop a set of study questions—of your own making or from the textbook they use—and give these to students prior to reading, taking time to discuss them, and perhaps make some predictions about what they think they know about them. Also, if the questions include unfamiliar vocabulary, this is an opportunity to address key terms and concepts before students read.

- Gather a collection of quotations related to a subject, and then ask students to read them and choose the one that interests them the most. In a senior class, students reading *Antigone* get a handout with ten quotations about different conceptions of the law from such thinkers as Martin Luther King, Jr., Socrates, and Oliver Wendell Holmes. We use these as the basis for discussion prior to beginning the play, focusing on the difference between human laws and divine laws.

- Create a set of statements about a subject (e.g., evil, morality, family, nature) that students all know something about and about which they have something to say. For example, for the *Lord of the Flies*, I stated "The man who dropped the bomb on Hiroshima is evil." Students had to agree or disagree, explaining their thinking. This is all a means of preparing the class to read and think about the problem of evil in the novel, and it gives us a way to frame our thinking by allowing us to formulate a continuum or set of criteria for evil.

Model.

Little needs to be said about what modeling means or why to do it. We all understand the logic of showing students what a successful performance looks like. Yes, it takes time to model, but this step seems essential if our students are to learn what we teach. Here are some key ways to provide effective but efficient models for students:

- Integrate the model into the handout you create. Whether you are creating the assignment yourself and need to prepare a sample for them to use, or are using materials created by a publisher, you can include a model to guide them. While it is best to discuss this model, doing a think-aloud about how students should complete the work, it is essential to at least provide them with a model to read.

- Demonstrate the lesson, activity, process, or skill for the class when introducing the lesson. The process is simple: I do, we do, then they do. I routinely copy to a transparency any handouts I use, including graphic organizers or other tools, and then put these on the overhead so students can see what I am doing. I then model for them how to use the tool and do the technique when reading.

- Show them how you want them to read if you are asking them to read in a particular way. If, for example, I want them to read for allusions, I model for students how I do this, using questions I ask myself.

- Create your own examples of assignments in front of the class to model the process of doing the activity. For example, if I want them to take notes while reading using a particular technique (e.g., Cornell notes), I put a transparency of the note-taking organizer on the overhead and read, then interrupt myself to take notes on that same sheet, telling them what I am writing and why.

- Copy student examples to use for current or future students. If I want students to learn how to annotate a text, for example, I copy a sample from a student who has done it very well and then provide that example to students the next year, explaining what the student did to get that result.

Perform Texts.

Combining several of the techniques outlined in this chapter, performance offers a blend of words, images, and gestures that help students understand what they are reading. The teacher can perform or the students can take it over, translating the dull page into vivid, descriptive movement that helps everyone better understand what the author means. It is a more active, fun-oriented technique, but no less serious than the others. I have found the following approaches engage readers and help them understand what we read:

- Readers Theater offers students the chance to adapt the text to a spoken performance of it, the emphasis falling on *how* to speak the words to evoke the characters and emotions. This method is particularly helpful as students don't need costumes, but must only prepare the text and their reading of it.

- *Tableau vivant* (French for "living picture") is an unspoken method of performing a text in which a group of students arrange themselves in a dramatic form that conveys the meaning of a scene. This method would apply well to a scene students read in a history textbook (e.g., the founders arguing over independence) as well as to a chapter about decisions in a health textbook.

- Video offers a variation on adapting a text to performance. Many students are interested in this approach as it allows them to apply their growing passion for film; for example, a student might create a movie of a poem in which actors interpret and perform its meaning.

- Dramatic interpretations and adaptations of literary works are common but powerful. A theatrical group called Word for Word takes short stories and performs them, speaking every word (even the "he said" or "she angrily demanded" tag lines) as they move about the stage.

- Musical performances never fail to amaze me as students turn Shakespearean sonnets into raps or set the sonnets to music with flutes and clarinets while readers act out the poem.

References

Bacevich, A., & Salinger, T. (2006) *Lessons and recommendations from the Alabama Reading Initiative: Sustaining focus on secondary reading.* Washington, DC: American Institutes for Research.

Baker, T. N., Wilhelm, J. D., & Hackett, J. B. (2001). *Strategic reading: Guiding students to lifelong literacy, 6–12.* Portsmouth, NH: Heinemann.

Beck, I., McKeown, M. G., Hamilton, R. L., & Kucan, L. (1997). *Questioning the author: An approach for enhancing student engagement with text.* Newark, DE: International Reading Association.

Beck, I. L., & McKeown, M. G. (2006) *Improving comprehension with questioning the author: A fresh and expanded view of a powerful approach.* New York, NY: Scholastic.

Biancarosa, C., & Snow, C. E. (2006). *Reading next: A vision for action and research in middle and high school literacy: A report to Carnegie Corporation of New York* (2nd ed.). Washington, DC: Alliance for Excellent Education.

Burke, J. (2002). *Tools for thought: Graphic organizers for your classroom.* Portsmouth, NH: Heinemann.

Heller, R., & Greenleaf, C. (2007). *Literacy instruction in the content areas: Getting to the core of middle and high school improvement.* Washington, DC: Alliance for Excellent Education.

Jensen, E. (2005). *Teaching with the brain in mind.* (2nd. ed.). Alexandria, VA: Association of Supervision and Curriculum Development.

Langer, J. A. (1981). From theory to practice: A pre-reading plan. *Journal of Reading, 25,* 152–156.

National Adolescent Literacy Coalition. (2007). *Foundational and emergent questions: Smart people talk about adolescent literacy.* Washington, DC: Author.

National Council of Teachers of English. (2006). *NCTE principles of adolescent literacy reform: A policy research brief.* Urbana, IL: Author.

Ogle, D. M. (1992). KWL in action: Secondary teachers find applications that work. In E. K. Dishner, T. W. Bean, J. E. Readance, & D. W. Moore (Eds.), *Reading in the content areas: Improving classroom instruction* (3rd ed., pp. 270–281). Dubuque, IA: Kendall-Hunt.

Palinscar, A. S., & Brown, A. L. (1984). Reciprocal teaching of comprehension-fostering and monitoring activities. *Cognition and Instruction, 1,* 117–175.

Rafael, T. E. (1986). Teaching question-answer relationships. *Reading Teacher, 36,* 516–520.

Vacca, R. T., & Vacca, J. L. (2005). *Content area reading: Literacy and learning across the curriculum.* (8th ed.). Boston: Pearson.

Willis, J. (2006). *Research-based strategies to ignite student learning.* Alexandria, VA: Association of Supervision and Curriculum Development.